JIM CROW AND ME

To: Jumba

Best Wishes !!!

Solomon S. Seay Jr

6 - 9 - 2010

Jim Crow, the system of laws and customs that enforced racial segregation and discrimination throughout the United States, especially the South, from the late nineteenth century to the 1960s. Signs reading "Whites Only" or "Colored" hung over drinking fountains and the doors to restrooms, restaurants, movie theaters, and other public places. Along with segregation, blacks, particularly in the South, faced discrimination in jobs and housing and were often denied their constitutional right to vote. Whether by law or by custom, all these obstacles to equal status went by the name Jim Crow. Jim Crow was the name of a character in minstrelsy (in which white performers in blackface used African American stereotypes in their songs and dances); it is not clear how the term came to describe American segregation and discrimination. Jim Crow has its origins in a variety of sources, including the Black Codes imposed upon African Americans immediately after the Civil War and prewar racial segregation of railroad cars in the North. But it was not until after Radical Reconstruction ended in 1877 that Jim Crow was born.

— EXCERPTED FROM *Africana: The Encyclopedia of the African and African American Experience*, KWAME ANTHONY APPIAH AND HENRY LOUIS GATES, JR., EDS.

JIM CROW AND ME

Stories from My Life as a Civil Rights Lawyer

SOLOMON S. SEAY, JR.

WITH DELORES R. BOYD

FOREWORD BY JOHN HOPE FRANKLIN

NEWSOUTH BOOKS

Montgomery | Louisville

NewSouth Books
105 South Court Street
Montgomery, AL 36104

Published in the United States by NewSouth Books, a division of NewSouth, Inc.,
Montgomery, Alabama.

Library of Congress Cataloging-in-Publication Data

Seay, Solomon S., 1931–
Jim Crow and me : stories from my life as a civil rights lawyer / Solomon S. Seay, Jr. ;
with Delores R. Boyd ; foreword by John Hope Franklin.
p. cm.
Includes bibliographical references and index.

ISBN-13: 978-1-58838-175-0
ISBN-10: 1-58838-175-7

1. African Americans—Civil rights—Alabama—History—20th century. 2. Civil
rights movements—Alabama—History—20th century. 3. African Americans—Legal
status, laws, etc.—Alabama—History—20th century. 4. African Americans—Segregation—Alabama—History. 5. Seay, Solomon S., 1931- 6. African American civil
rights workers—Biography. 7. African American lawyers—Biography. 8. Seay, S. S.
(Solomon Snowden), 1899-1988—Family. 9. Racism—Alabama—History—20th
century. 10. Alabama—Race relations—History—20th century. I. Boyd, Delores R.
II. Title.
E185.93.A3S43 2008
323.1196'0730761—dc22

2008034340

Design by Randall Williams

Printed in the United States of America
by the Maple-Vail Book Manufacturing Group

Solomon S. Seay, Sr., 1899–1988

TO THE MEMORY OF MY FATHER,

THE REVEREND SOLOMON SNOWDEN SEAY, SR.

AND TO THE MEMORY OF MY WIFE,

ETTRA SPENCER SEAY

AND ALSO FOR THE INSPIRATION OF

A WHALE THAT I NEVER SAW

ETTRA

(DECEMBER 21, 1933–MAY 28, 2006)

Always for me, beside me,
    because of me.

My will, my way, my voice,
    my needs, my choice.

Your dreams deferred
    for mine . . .
    they did not rot,
    you did not explode . . .

No festering sores
    ever scarred your soul.

From your heart flowed
    endless love,
    precious love,
    only love.

Empowering, sustaining, and forgiving
    me . . . ours . . .
    somebody's child.

For your faithfulness . . .
    I am here.

— SOL

Laws for racial segregation had made a brief appearance during Reconstruction, only to disappear by 1868. When the Conservatives resumed power, they revived the segregation of the races. Beginning in Tennessee in 1870, white Southerners enacted laws against intermarriage of the races in every Southern state. Five years later, Tennessee adopted the first "Jim Crow" law, and the rest of the South rapidly fell in line. Blacks and whites were separated on trains, in depots, and on wharves. After the Supreme Court in 1883 outlawed the Civil Rights Act of 1875, the Negro was banned from white hotels, barber shops, restaurants, and theaters. By 1885 most Southern states had laws requiring separate schools. With the adoption of new constitutions the states firmly established the color line by the most stringent separation of the races; and in 1896 the Supreme Court upheld segregation in its "separate but equal" doctrine set forth in *Plessy v. Ferguson*.

—EXCERPTED FROM *From Slavery to Freedom: A History of Negro Americans*, BY JOHN HOPE FRANKLIN AND ALFRED A. MOSS, JR.

CONTENTS

Foreword by John Hope Franklin / XI

Preface by Solomon S. Seay, Jr. / XIV

Introduction by Delores R. Boyd / XVII

PART ONE: INSPIRATION FOR THE BATTLEFIELD

1 — The Whale I Did Not See / 5

2 — Miss Arter's Pledge of Allegiance / 8

PART TWO: JIM CROW'S PRIVILEGES

3 — Passing the Bar / 11

4 — They Must Have Been Brothers / 14

5 — Biding Time at The Elite / 21

6 — Bye Bye Blackbird / 23

7 — The Color of Convenience / 29

PART THREE: LIBERTY AND JUSTICE
FOR THOSE WHO GOT THE GUTS TO GRAB IT

8 — Saving PeeWee / 33

9 — Facing Fear / 40

10 — A Promise Kept / 45

11 — I Cried Real Tears / 48

12 — A Widow's Might / 54

13 — Fools Profit from Their Own Mistakes / 57

Part Four: Fearless Freedom Fighters

14 — The Turkey Bone Warriors / 63

15 — Cottonreader and the Chinaberry Tree / 69

16 — Bert & Dan . . . and the Ku Klux Klan / 74

17 — The Other Side of the Battle / 79

18 — Freedom Riders and a Slow Delivery / 82

19 — Marengo County / 89

Part Five: All In the Family

20 — What's In a Name? / 101

21 — Plowing with Pride / 104

22 — Never a Mumbling Word / 108

23 — Flute Lips / 110

24 — The Lake House / 116

Part Six: Judging the Journey

25 — Reputation / 123

26 — Tolerated Injustice / 129

Notes / 134

Index / 148

FOREWORD

John Hope Franklin

As one who lived through the Civil Rights Movement and who participated in it on a limited basis, I am delighted to cheer along the Seay-Boyd collaboration. This is, indeed, an exciting joint effort, not unlike the project my son and I worked together when we published my father's autobiography, *My Life and an Era*. It is virtually impossible to portray that period unless one had a special prism through which to view it or, at least, a vantage point from which to consider its momentous events.

I am surprised at the number of people who have, somehow, associated me with the day-to-day developments in the Tulsa, Oklahoma, race riots of late May and early June of 1921. I was not in Tulsa at the time and would not arrive there for the first time until May or June 1925. Meanwhile, my mother, younger sister, and I survived the suspense of not knowing for three or four weeks if my father was alive or among the charred bodies that lay on the roadways for days and even weeks after the shooting and looting had ceased. My older sister and brother were away in a boarding high school in Tennessee. When my mother, sister, and I reached Tulsa from Rentiesville in 1925, I was ten years old and in the seventh grade. My father, whose law practice was better than it had been when he moved to Tulsa just before the riot, was overjoyed that the family was together again.

As I read of the remarkable account of Solomon Seay's struggles against Jim Crow in Alabama, I could not resist seeing the striking similarity that they bore to my father's struggles in Oklahoma. Like Seay, my father fought Jim Crow whenever and wherever he found it. One notable example was the city ordinance against the use of certain flammable materials in construction, a sure effort to block rebuilding by poverty stricken blacks. My father took the case of one of his disobedient clients to the state supreme court, where the ordinance was declared unconstitutional. Then, there were the long afternoons I spent with him in his office, where there were few clients and I had an abundance of homework. I almost wished that clients would stay away, which would give me my father's exclusive attention, even if it meant that he collected no fees from the very few clients who could afford to pay.

I do not believe that my dad ever met Solomon Seay, and the closest I got to him was in 1943 when I taught in the summer session of Montgomery's Alabama State College. It was the year that I saw patterns of segregation that must have strained the imagination of its creators. The most notable of these was at the state liquor store, where the line leading up to the counter was divided by a wooden wall; but the sales counter itself was common for both races, so that a single clerk could serve people on both sides of the racial divide.

It does not take more than a few minutes of scrutiny to discover that racial segregation represents one of the most creative and imaginative pursuits ever improvised by mankind. Even if the creative spirit was alive and well in shaping the sale and distribution of alcoholic beverages, it was no more creative than some of its contemporaneous colleagues whose creative imagination would doubtless be strained at times in making certain that the races would remain segregated.

I am delighted that Attorney Seay and Delores Boyd have decided to share their experiences with the general public. Her courage as well as her resourcefulness and ingenuity made his life a rich resource for all of us to emulate. For groups that have not yet broken the back of segregation in their lives and experiences, the battle of the Seays and Boyds is an ideal place to begin their own battle against racial segregation in their own lives.

John Hope Franklin (1915–) is a United States historian and past president of the American Historical Association. Professor Emeritus of History at Duke University, he is best known for his work From Slavery to Freedom, *first published in 1947, and continuously updated. More than three million copies have been sold. In 1995, he was awarded the Presidential Medal of Freedom, the nation's highest civilian honor.*

PREFACE

Solomon S. Seay, Jr.

I scheduled an early morning flight from Montgomery to Greensboro, North Carolina. The night before, sleep escaped me well beyond the midnight hour even though I had missed my afternoon nap. I tossed and turned but, eyes wide open or shut, the whale splashed tauntingly into view—an unusually large whale with the number 1743 emblazoned across his gaping jaw.

Was I asleep enough to dream?

The image of the whale appeared and disappeared, first with and then without the glittering number 1743.

Finally, that huge whale—this time with the number shining on his gigantic tale fin—dived deep into the ocean and disappeared. Immediately I fell into a restful sleep.

Early the next morning, a long-lost memory startled me awake. I recalled the precise address—1743 McConnell Road—of my childhood home in Greensboro, and I saw myself walking from that house, along with my two brothers and our father, to see a whale at a street-corner carnival three miles away.

The Whale I Did Not See introduces this book and captures the greatest lesson my father ever taught me.

THE FLIGHT TO GREENSBORO passed over the city of Salisbury and the little town of Sedalia. I spent my undergraduate years in Salisbury at Livingstone College. Just a stone's throw away, an internationally renowned boarding school, Palmer Memorial Institute, graced the piney woods of Sedalia. Palmer's brilliant black founder, Charlotte Hawkins Brown, was often called "The First Lady of Social Graces."

In the 1940s and 1950s, Livingstone, Palmer, and all other historically black schools in the Carolinas, the District of Columbia, Maryland, Virginia, Georgia, and Alabama recessed early, and on the same day, for the Christmas holidays. Students welcomed the long break to earn money in seasonal jobs, and the train ride back home made for memorable mingling.

The trains then were as segregated as all public transportation in the South, but only on the train did black passengers get to sit up front. The only "colored" seating on each train was always the first passenger coach behind the engine. It was a dubious honor, to say the least: with burning coal or wood powering the train, soot and ashes emitted by tall smoke stacks settled largely on the first coach—not air-conditioned, of course.

ON THE EVENING OF Christmas break 1948, when the train reached Salisbury, the colored coach overflowed with students. I took a seat on the aisle floor, with my saxophone case as a cushion.

When I thought everyone had fallen asleep, I eased my way to the private coach reserved for Palmer students only, all the way to New Orleans. Vacant seats were plentiful, and I sat next to the most fascinating young lady I had ever met. She displayed all of the poise and grace which distinguished Palmer girls; and she had the most dazzling eyes! I gazed deeply and with unabashed pleasure into eyes which looked like the clear bottom of a deep artesian well.

An intriguing look I would never forget!

Even though I was hooked on modern jazz, I did recall one or two romantic sonatas and foolishly tuned my saxophone to serenade her softly. Needless to say, I managed only to get kicked out of the Palmer coach . . . but not before I matched a name with those eyes: Ettra Spencer, from Galveston, Texas.

As I returned to my seat on my sax case in the colored coach, I knew that somehow—somewhere—we would meet again and she would become a part of me.

SEVERAL YEARS LATER, WHILE sitting on the bleachers in the gym at Howard University, I glimpsed again those dazzling eyes as she went up for a "crip shot" on the basketball court. I knew then and there that my destiny had been revealed. On August 16, 1953, Ettra and I were joined in Holy Matrimony.

Sometimes I lovingly referred to Ettra as "Skipper" because she was indeed the ship's master, my little sine qua non.

Because of the deep and abiding influences that each had on my life and career, this book is dedicated to my dad, Reverend Solomon Snowden Seay, Sr., whose struggle for civil rights transcended all else; to my loving wife "Skipper," without whom I feel empty; and to that whale I did not see.

INTRODUCTION

Delores R. Boyd

My unfulfilled dream—to practice law with Solomon Seay—would have been a nightmare. I can say that now with certainty and without angst. Wrong time (mid-1970s), wrong gender (mine), and wrong personality (his).

It took more than a decade for someone in the know to disclose the untold truth of my rejection in 1976 by the venerable law firm of Gray, Langford, and Seay: partner Seay (he pronounces it "See") just did not think a young woman could keep up with his busy civil rights practice stretched across Alabama's highways and byways.

Ironically, it took his father, Reverend Solomon S. Seay (he pronounced it "Say") so little time to discern in my youth the inner vision and steely strength which catapulted me easily through college and law school. He would have told his son to hire me in a heartbeat. So would his sister, Hagalyn Seay Wilson, M.D., with whom I shared a birth date (minus twenty years) and more until her death in 2006.

Reverend Seay and Dr. Wilson mentored me from seventh grade through high-school graduation. I didn't call it mentoring then. It was work. On the weekday afternoon not designated for after-school piano or typing and shorthand lessons, I left Loveless Junior High School on West Jeff Davis Avenue and walked right across the street to Dr. Wilson's office. Always crowded with patients, children, and clutter, the office introduced me to the unique tribulations of a strong, fiercely black and fiercely independent woman, wed till death did them part to a husband, a professional calling, and six children whose parenting she refused to compromise. The little tasks she assigned me—filing, typing, cleaning, babysitting—mattered less than the priceless opportunities to watch her in action and partake of her wisdom.

My times with Reverend Seay were less structured but no less instructive. Our families were bonded by the African Methodist Episcopal Zion Church and the Montgomery Improvement Association (MIA). He followed Dr. Martin Luther King and Reverend Ralph Abernathy as president of the MIA, and his was the reliably calm and spiritually profound voice in the strategic planning which preceded not only the Montgomery Bus Boycott but also the desegregation of public schools and public accommodations.

My typing skills provided the perfect excuse for our interactions; whether leaving a manuscript for typing or securing my finished product, he held me captive for what seemed like hours. Our provocative conversations belied our age gap and seemed perfectly natural in the powerful times which shaped my childhood between 1957, at age seven, through high-school graduation in 1968.

I grew up as "child" of the movement and when I graduated from Loveless in 1965, I had not missed even a handful of the MIA's weekly mass meetings. The most memorable lasted through the night at First Baptist Church on a May evening in 1961 after a mob assaulted a busload of Freedom Riders. We rallied inside to support their cause while another mob of belligerent whites taunted on the outside.

FRED GRAY FREQUENTLY REPORTED at MIA meetings on legal battles being waged by him with law partners Sol Seay and Charles Langford. I don't recall any interactions at all with Sol before I left home for college, but I carried with me his image and reputation for the legal career I envisioned before I reached adolescence.

Barely two years after my rejection by the Gray, Seay, & Langford firm, I stood toe-to-toe against Sol before the venerated Frank M. Johnson, Jr., United States District Judge, in the federal courthouse which now honors his great legacy. It had been Sol's second home for twenty years as he waged successful battles against racial segregation and criminal injustices throughout the state. By contrast, I never stepped foot inside the courthouse—save for postal business on the first floor—until 1974, when John C. Godbold, then a judge on the United States Court of Appeals for the Fifth Circuit, interviewed me as a potential law clerk.

Armed only with my University of Virginia legal training and a year's clerkship with Judge Godbold, I tried my first, and most controversial, discrimination lawsuit. Because I had dreamed this occasion would find me teamed with Sol, I did not savor my ultimate victory.

While I matured in a challenging law practice between 1976 and 2001, Sol's stature also heightened, as did my genuine respect for him. Long after many stalwarts in the civil rights bar gravitated to more lucrative practices, Sol's tenacity simply amazed me. It also earned him the respect of bar and bench, irrespective of race, ideology, or client base.

It is virtually impossible to find any black lawyer in practice during the 1970s for whom Sol Seay is not a revered trailblazer. He is similarly esteemed in the national bar of civil rights lawyers. The NAACP Legal Defense Fund routinely associated Sol in significant litigation to vindicate constitutional rights for criminal defendants and equal opportunities for African Americans.

No lawyer in the state of Alabama devoted more time continuously to the cause of dismantling segregation in public schools. Just as a core group of his Howard Law School professors painstakingly designed the strategic underpinnings of *Brown v. Board of Education*, Sol teamed with Fred Gray to attack school segregation many years after *Brown*'s mandate. As resistance to school integration re-surfaced in many disingenuous forms over four decades, Sol kept battling in the enforcement arena until 1998.

Sol's presence and demeanor can be intimidating. Like his father, he says what he means to say and leaves no doubt that he means what he says. Racism, inequality, and injustice are unacceptable evils to him, and both mother and father instilled his inclination to resist them.

In mid-1999, I volunteered to interview Sol for an archival project to honor distinguished lawyers and judges in the United States District Court for the Middle District of Alabama. I conducted two informal interviews before recording, on June 30, 2000, the archived interview. A few months later Sol finally succumbed to my incessant begging and shared with me some of his narratives about memorable episodes in his early practice. I determined immediately that his stories had to be told.

I ventured initially to document the "big picture" story of the mere handful of black lawyers with private law practices in the capital city between 1957, when Sol started, and 1959: Fred Gray, Charles Langford, Calvin Pryor, and Charles Conley. After meeting Mahala Ashley Dickerson, the first black woman with a law practice in Montgomery following her 1948 admission to the bar, I planned to include her remarkable story. Incredibly vibrant in her eighties and still practicing law, then in Alaska, she self-published in 1991 her autobiography, *Delayed Justice for Sale*.

Soon I acknowledged my sheer inability to pursue well and simultaneously this ambitious task, a full-time solo law practice, and part-time service as Presiding Judge for the Montgomery Municipal Court. I readily narrowed the scope of this book when Sol agreed to let me be his storyteller. In September 2001, I left the active practice of law for a merit appointment as a United States Magistrate Judge for the Middle District of Alabama. I tried in vain to keep the book on the front burner. Only after I stepped down from the bench, at the end of 2006, did I undertake in earnest this delightful challenge.

"I HAVE NO INTEREST in putting together an autobiography," Sol cautioned me during our initial planning session four years earlier.

"I hate to see history distorted," he explained, "that's why I stopped going to movies."

Many of the working titles for the two dozen stories in the binder Sol handed me aroused my curiosity immediately: "Political Trickery"; "Flute Lips"; "I Cried Real Tears"; "That Sweet Old Widow Woman"; "My First Experience with the Plantation System"; and "She Never Said a Mumbling Word."

Sol described as "disjointed episodes" the stories about his memorable trials and incidents between 1957 and 1977. Some are "light and lively, but others are quite serious." He envisioned a book which would be enjoyed by non-lawyers as well as lawyers: "Anyone should be able to pick up the book and start with any episode, put the book down, and come back to read another story, anywhere in the book. I want the reader first to enjoy what he's reading—to do no more than to experience vicariously some of the things that I experienced as a black civil rights lawyer in Alabama. If the episode is about a protest of certain conditions, I want the reader to find himself, in effect, living those protest moments and developing a feel for the fight. I want some stories to have some meaning yet while being entertaining."

SOL ALREADY HAD A title in mind, "The Whale I Did Not See." Responding to my quizzical stare, he recounted in riveting detail his father's principled stand for equal treatment from a racist circus vendor in the 1930s. This inspiring tale introduces this collection.

I created anew three additional stories—a short tribute to one of Sol's primary teachers, a perspective on his experience with the bar exam, and the concluding story. The rest started with Sol's narratives. Each of my ambitious rewrites emerged after our independent reviews of case and historical records as well as voluminous discussions to clarify facts and contexts.

To fulfill Sol's desire that the reader feel his experiences, I enlivened his recollections, wherever practical, with a storyteller's active voice and dialogue not intended to reflect verbatim accuracy. In each such instance, however, I corroborated the substantial veracity of attributed statements by reference to some reliable record (e.g., an official or published case, exhibit, article, or book), Sol's positive memory, or his recollection refreshed after poring over case files stored in various courthouse basements and in the Alabama Department of Archives and History.

Many lawyers who have interacted with Sol during his lengthy practice fondly recall some memorable incident which is "telling" about his character as a determined champion of civil rights. "I just hope he tells the Todd Road story," a Montgomery lawyer told me.

Another asked, "Did he tell you about the trials here in Montgomery before *Sullivan v. New York Times* reached the United States Supreme Court?"

Yes, these stories and countless more could be shared. In the end, I opted to stay with the stories Sol penned contemporaneously. They illustrate best the courage of this lawyer who dared to get in, and stay in, the civil rights battleground when it was lonely, unpopular, and dangerous.

Our twenty-sixth president, Theodore Roosevelt, penned in 1910:

> It is not the critic who counts; not the man who points out how the strong man stumbles, or where the doer of deeds could have done them better. The credit belongs to the man who is actually in the arena, whose face is marred by dust and sweat and blood; who strives valiantly; who errs, who comes short again and again, because there is no effort without error and shortcoming; but who does actually strive to do the deeds; who knows great enthusiasms, the great devotions; who spends himself in a worthy cause; who at the best knows in the end the triumph of high achievement, and who at the worst, if he fails, at least fails while daring greatly, so that his place shall never be with those cold and timid souls who neither know victory nor defeat.

Much credit belongs to Solomon S. Seay, Jr., and it is my fervent hope that his legacy as a civil rights lawyer will inspire generations to the cause of "liberty and justice for all."

Jim Crow and Me

Part One

Inspiration for the Battlefield

"When you follow in the path of your father,
you learn to walk like him."

— *Ashanti proverb*

I

THE WHALE I DID NOT SEE

Aman thrown overboard from a ship into a raging sea, swallowed by a giant fish, and spit out—whole and alive—after three days and three nights. That's the story of Jonah I swallowed in Sunday School.

My eyes must have bulged when I saw the whale in an advertisement for the circus coming to Greensboro, North Carolina. Daddy promised to take me and my two younger brothers to see the whale. My little mind did not ponder how a live whale could be carted around on dry land with a traveling circus. Nor did I wonder how Jonah stayed alive inside that whale.

The anticipation was almost too much for an eight-year-old preacher's kid nurtured on more Bible stories than I could count. When the day finally came, we walked almost three miles from our house. Nobody complained.

At the entrance to the tent show a white man collected admission fees. Now, more than six decades later, I remember the next scene as if it happened just yesterday.

Daddy put a bill in the man's hand. It could have been a dollar bill, probably not much more for an attraction like this in the late 1930s. The man took the bill and, ignoring my father's outstretched hand, threw his change on top of the counter.

Daddy kept holding out his hand. Staring straight at the man,

5

Daddy spoke without fear: "Sir, would you put my change in my hand the way I put my money in your hand?"

"Do you want your money, boy?" If this snarling challenge didn't intimidate Daddy, my brothers and I definitely felt the heat as we cowered ever so slightly behind him.

"Yes, sir." My daddy's steadfast glare left no doubt about his equally resolute conviction. "I just want you to put my change in my hand like I put my money in your hand."

The change stayed put on the counter, and the drama continued.

"If you want your change, boy, you better get it."

"No, sir," Daddy replied, "if you can't put my change in my hand, you give me my money back."

Disgusted and—to his surprise—defeated, the man handed over the bill my father had tendered. He would forfeit the profits from four admission tickets before giving in to a black man's polite request for treatment in kind.

Daddy turned away brusquely. He grabbed my hand and cradled his arm around my brothers. "Come on boys, let's go home."

I cannot say now that I understood then. I did not. I was angry, hurt, and about as disappointed as I ever was in my youth.

My father's silence on the long walk home left me confused and afraid to complain. He never said a word about the incident then or thereafter. No explanation, no apology, no moral.

I never found out if that whale appeared live as advertised. I moped around the house for a long time grieving my lost opportunity of a lifetime.

I had grown into a man the age my father was then when I pieced together his lesson.

As I sat by his dying bedside many decades later, I reminded him of that time, hoping he would recall the moment and explain himself. He did not remember.

When he asked me if I ever gave any thought to writing about my times as a civil rights lawyer, I quickly replied, "I sure have, and I know exactly what I'm going to call it: *The Whale*."

I told him that his showdown with the ticket-taker at the whale show empowered me and continues to guide my path as a civil rights lawyer.

He did not try to hide his tears.

I knew he remembered.

2

MISS ARTER'S PLEDGE OF ALLEGIANCE

In Knoxville, Tennessee, Miss A. O. Arter summoned my junior high school class to attention each morning to stand and recite the Pledge of Allegiance. State law required all public schools to begin the day with the same ritual. With hands over hearts and eyes on the American Flag, we followed her lead:

"I pledge allegiance to the flag of the United States of America and to the Republic for which it stands: one nation, under God, indivisible, with liberty and justice . . ."

At this point Miss Arter's voice always resonated above ours.

We said: "*For all.*"

She proclaimed, each time: "*For those who got the guts to grab it!*"

She never explained her substitution; nor did she urge us to follow her lead.

I became a civil rights lawyer, Miss Arter.

I heard you.

Part Two

Jim Crow's Privileges

"The first faults are theirs that commit them;
the second faults, theirs that permit them."

3

PASSING THE BAR

The University of Alabama established a school of law in 1872. Three years later the Alabama Supreme Court granted all graduates a "diploma privilege" to practice law in Alabama without taking any kind of examination. In 1897 the Alabama legislature preserved the privilege by requiring non-graduates to pass a written bar examination.[1]

A "whites-only" policy controlled admissions to the University until June 11, 1963, when Governor George C. Wallace staged his infamous "stand in the schoolhouse door." Because Vivian Malone and James Hood stood taller and waltzed through the door, blacks integrated the law school about five years later.

The University's law school stood as Alabama's only accredited law school until Cumberland moved its private law school from Tennessee to Birmingham in 1961. Rather than extend to Cumberland law graduates the "diploma privilege" enjoyed by University of Alabama law graduates, the state abolished the privilege altogether.[2]

Like so many other privileges a segregated America bestowed on whites, the diploma privilege happened to disappear around the same time blacks appeared poised to partake.[3]

For almost two decades before desegregation at Alabama's public law school, the state doggedly financed segregation by subsidizing legal education for blacks at out-of-state law schools.[4] (Alabama blacks seeking education for careers in medicine, dentistry, and other professions received similar out-of-state opportunities.) And so it was that the Alabama state treasury paid for my tuition and living expenses at Howard Law School in Washington, D.C., starting in 1952.

Chartered by the U.S. Congress in 1867 as a historically black college, Howard opened its law school two years later. By the middle of the twentieth century it had become the nation's best training ground for civil rights lawyers. Led by Charles Hamilton Houston, its venerable Harvard-educated dean, Howard Law School attracted the best and brightest legal scholars. My professors included architects of the landmark decision in *Brown v. Board of Education*, 347 U.S. 483 (1954).

After a year of law school, I put aside law books and trudged in army boots for two years. Law degree finally in hand, I came home to Montgomery in the summer of 1957. Joined by my law school classmate, Calvin S. Pryor, I prepared to take the bar examination that University of Alabama law graduates then had the privilege to bypass.[5]

We sat with seventeen whites—also graduates of out-of-state law schools—for the three-day essay examination covering sixteen subjects. All the candidates had assigned numbers; not surprisingly, mine was #18 while Calvin received #19.

Bar administrators recommended to the white applicants a popular spot for lunch inside the downtown building. Calvin and I were taken outside and directed to "a very good colored restaurant" three blocks away. They had no idea that Calvin's uncle owned the place and had given him a generous ownership interest to congratulate him on finishing law school.

I passed the bar exam on the first round. Calvin did not. I remain confident that his initial failure had more to do with his "number" than with his actual performance.

While I proceeded to set up my law office, Calvin prepared to hear his "number" called at the next sitting for the bar. He did, and he went on to cap off a successful solo practice with an illustrious career as the first black appointed an assistant U.S. attorney in Alabama's federal courts.

4

They Must Have Been Brothers

September 15, 1957. A convenient shortcut from home to work at Jackson Hospital took the sixteen-year-old Mark Gilmore right through the center of Oak Park, the city's oldest public park.

His mother's home had been a regular stopping place for the leaders and workers who kept the Montgomery Bus Boycott strong for over a year; her down-home cooking was the main attraction. He often listened in on the strategy sessions.

Protest was not on his mind that autumn afternoon. He simply didn't want to be late for the job which meant a few extra dollars to fulfill a teenager's whims. And so, the familiar shortcut through the stunningly beautiful park—forty wooded acres of gardens and playgrounds, swimming pool, picnic quarters, duck pond, and petting zoo with goats, sheep, peacocks, and Australian Red Rabbits.

Mark usually managed to make the quick walk-through without incident. Not so this time. An angry policeman spotted him almost immediately, and after a gratuitous beating, took him straight to jail. It would be his home for almost two weeks before his trial for violating the city ordinance which segregated Oak Park and every other city park or recreational facility.[6]

About the same time of Mark's trial and predictable conviction in October 1957, I received my license to practice law in the state of Alabama. A few months later his mother cornered me in the corridors of the Montgomery County Courthouse. She got right down to business after I greeted her as the "lunch lady for the Bus Protest."

Gazing on me from head to toe, she said, "Son, you are going to be a good lawyer, but we want you to look like a lawyer."

As I glanced down at my dress shirt, brightly colored tie, sports coat, contrasting slacks, and white bucks, she told me that she worked for the owner of The Hub, a top-end men's clothing store downtown. "I got good credit with him," she went on, "and I want you to tell him I sent you to be outfitted with a dark dress suit and black dress shoes."

"Thank you, ma'am." I politely ended our little chat knowing full well that I could not afford even to peep inside the store, let alone to obligate myself for the value of a Hub dress suit and shoes.

I DOUBT THAT I had upgraded my wardrobe much by the time Mrs. Gilmore contacted me to do something about Mark's conviction for walking through Oak Park.

I started by submitting to the city's Parks and Recreation Board a petition, signed by Mrs. Gilmore and a significant number of the city's black residents, requesting an end to the official policy which denied "colored persons" the right to use the city's public parks. The board duly acknowledged receipt of the petition on August 25, 1958, but ducked action in deference to the city ordinance which mandated the policy.

Next stop: City Hall, on September 17. I ushered all of the petitioners and a host of supporters into the second-floor meeting room of the Montgomery City Commission. Two large double doors guarded the spacious room furnished with a conference table and several rows of long benches on either side of a center aisle.

We arrived early. Puzzled by the absence of the usual signs for racially separated seating, someone in our group asked me where they were supposed to sit. I jokingly replied, "At the back, if you are black." They all congregated in the rear benches on the right side of the aisle. Knowing we were first on the agenda, I took a seat in the middle of the first bench on the left side of the aisle, just in front of the commissioners' conference table.

When the commissioners entered the room, one of the three, Clyde Sellers, marched straight to my seat. Pointing to the other side of the aisle, he glared at me but spoke loudly enough for all to hear: "Niggers sit over there."

I kept sitting, stone-faced and silent, for at least a minute. Then I stood, slowly gathered my materials, and moved to the first chair in front of the conference table—directly in front of Sellers. When I sat down, he got up, walked out of the room, and stood in the doorway until I completed my presentation and all the blacks with me left the hearing room.

As we were leaving, we heard the unmistakably boastful last words from Mayor W. A. "Tacky" Gayle: "The commission will not operate integrated parks."

I HAD FAIR NOTICE that the commissioners' resistance would extend to closing the parks. Just days before the scheduled hearing I had been visited at my law office by a black man on a mission. I recognized him immediately as a paid emissary of the city's white establishment.

He toted an attaché case loaded with more cash than I could reasonably expect to earn in the next year or two as a black civil rights lawyer. Leaving the case completely open on my desk, he sat and calmly repeated the message sent with the cash.

"I know you have invested a lot of time and expense in pushing this parks issue," he started, "and I've come prepared to take care of these little problems so you can move on to something else." As I endured his lecture on how things are done in Montgomery, I thought about Abe Lincoln's reported reply to an adversary earnestly seeking to buy his support for a project: "Every man has his price, and you are getting dangerously close to mine."

But I also thought about a dress suit and shoes from The Hub.

While I would like to think that I turned down the case full of cash as a matter of good conscience and morality, in retrospect, I think it was really because I was just plain scared.

Before leaving my office the black emissary asked to use the telephone. "Tacky," he said in an exasperated tone, "this boy is young and dumb. We need to meet."

The city's black intermediary did have more success persuading the token blacks on the payroll at Parks and Recreation that my persistence would force the city to close the parks and leave them jobless. They wasted little time making public their plans to picket my office, and the local newspaper gratefully blessed the plan with a banner headline the next day: "Negroes call for a boycott of Seay's law office."

Bolstered by my clients' firm resolve, I ignored the intimidation and pressed on with the class action lawsuit filed in federal court on December 22, 1958. The case was titled:

Georgia Theresa Gilmore, Gussie Carlton, Sylvia Johnson, J. C. Smith, Mattie Cargill, Fred Harris, George Stephens, Elizabeth Brown, on behalf of themselves and all others similarly situated, Plaintiffs, v. City of Montgomery, Alabama, a Municipal Corporation; Board of Commissioners of the City of Montgomery; W. A. Gayle, Frank W. Parks

and Clyde C. Sellers, as Members of the Board of Commissioners of
the City of Montgomery; Parks and Recreation Board of the City of
Montgomery; Mrs. James Fitts Hill, Father M. J. Rafferty, Reverend
Louis Armstrong, Florian Strassburger, and Jack Hope, as Members
of the Parks and Recreation Board; T. A. Belser, as Superintendent
of the Parks and Recreational Program for the City of Montgomery,
Alabama, Defendants.[7]

We asked U.S. District Judge Frank M. Johnson, Jr. to declare
the ordinance unconstitutional and to enjoin the city from operating
racially segregated public parks. Promptly responding to the lawsuit,
the city commissioners adopted a resolution making the public parks
off-limits to everyone:

> Whereas eight negroes, namely, Georgia Theresa Gilmore, Gussie
> Carlton, Sylvia Johnson, J. C. Smith, Mattie Cargill, Fred Harris,
> George Stephens, and Elizabeth Brown, have attempted to compel
> the integration of Oak Park and other public parks in the City of
> Montgomery, hereinafter designated, by suit in the Federal District
> Court; and
> Whereas, this attempt poses grave problems involving the wel-
> fare and public safety of all the citizens of the City of Montgomery;
> and
> Whereas, the members of the Commission are of the opinion
> that it is to the best interest of the citizens of Montgomery that said
> parks be closed;
> Now, Therefore, Be It Resolved by the Board of Commissioners
> of the City of Montgomery, Alabama, that the following public parks
> in the City of Montgomery, to-wit, . . . be closed beginning January

1, 1959 to all persons, regardless of color, until further action of the Parks and Recreation Board and the Mayor and Commissioners of the City of Montgomery.[8]

The Parks and Recreation Board proceeded almost immediately to close Oak Park. They gathered up the ducks and geese from the duck pond; they removed the domestic animals from the petting zoo and trapped most of those roaming outside; and they filled the wading pool and the swimming pool with sand.

Arguing that closing all the parks effectively mooted the legal issues, the defendants filed a motion to dismiss the complaint. Judge Johnson denied the motion and decided the case based on the pleadings, stipulations, oral testimony, briefs, and arguments.

The evidence established only one instance (Mark Gilmore's) for trespassing by a Negro in an all-white park, but it left no doubt that the city intended to, and did, enforce the ordinance requiring citizens to use only the public parks set aside for their race. Judge Johnson readily concluded,

> that the policy, practice, custom and usage of denying to these Negro plaintiffs and members of the class they represent the right and privilege of admission to and use of any of the public parks owned, operated, supervised, and maintained by the City of Montgomery is a denial of these plaintiffs and members of the class they represent the equal protection of the laws as secured to them by the Fourteenth Amendment to the Constitution of the United States and such practice, policy, custom and usage is, therefore, unconstitutional.[9]

The opinion, issued on September 9, 1959, did not require the city to reopen the parks but instead enjoined it from reopening and operating them again on a segregated basis:

> It should now be made clear that all this Court now holds is simply that insofar as is legally required the City of Montgomery, Alabama, need not operate any public parks or make available to its citizens any recreational facilities; all public parks and all recreational facilities may remain closed for as long as the City—acting through its elected officials and agents—sees fit to keep them closed. However, when and if the parks are reopened as public parks each must be available for the benefit of all the public regardless of race or color upon a nondiscriminatory basis.[10]

Giving new meaning to a popular cigarette commercial of the time—"We'd rather fight than switch"—the city kept its public parks absolutely closed for almost nine years, until a totally reorganized city government in 1967 acted to reopen them on an integrated basis.

In their haste to round up all the animals and shut down Oak Park in 1959, Parks employees somehow missed two deer. Occasionally, a passerby peering through the fenced park could spy the deer playfully grazing or munching on the drooping foliage from the many trees and bushes which continued to blossom. Amazingly, those two deer were as fat, frisky, and free-spirited as ever when the Park gates opened again in late 1967.

Either they had been living in celibacy, or the two must have been brothers.

5

Biding Time at The Elite

F ederal litigation preoccupied just about my entire law practice
in the early years. During the frequent walks from my office to
the U.S. District Court, I passed right by the Elite (pronounced
e-light) Cafe.

An imposing fixture at the corner of Lee and Montgomery streets,
the Elite reigned for decades as the favorite lunch spot and evening
watering hole for the white establishment in legal, business, and government circles. Often I gazed at the attractive façade and wondered
when I might have the chance to see the interior.

July 2, 1964. After acrimonious filibusters orchestrated by Southern
senators and representatives, Congress finally passed the Civil Rights
Act of 1964. It easily ranked as the most sweeping civil rights legislation since Reconstruction. President Lyndon Johnson had scheduled
televised remarks for 6:45 P.M., when he was to sign the act into law.
The section banning segregation in restaurants and other places of
public accommodations would go into effect immediately.

As soon as I heard the news, I decided to be the first black to dine
at the Elite.

Around 5:30 P.M., I proudly opened the door to the Elite for an
evening meal with Ettra, our nine-year-old daughter Sheryl Denise,
and three-year-old Yalise Yvette. Our son Quinton Spencer, a month
or so shy of his first birthday, missed the occasion.

The elegant interior did not disappoint—white linen tablecloths and napkins, the full complement of etiquette-ordered glasses and silverware, and impeccably clad waiters. We were seated at a table near the center of the restaurant, with Yalise in her own little booster chair and a cute linen bib.

Comfortably seated and surprisingly relaxed, we waited. Several minutes passed while we watched waiters scurrying about to serve a number of white patrons who arrived well after our grand entrance. Finally I got a waiter's attention and asked to speak with the manager.

A distinguished-looking gentleman came to the table. "May I help you?" He seemed oblivious to our state.

I demanded to know if they intended to serve us.

In a polite, matter-of-fact tone, he related his understanding that the president would sign the new law at 6:20 P.M., Alabama time. We would be served at 6:20 P.M., and not one minute before, he added.

So we waited.

Ettra and I chatted nonstop during the wait and hardly noticed Yalise's antics to get our attention until she blurted out loudly, "Daddy, I dropped my rag."

That embarrassing moment prompted our pledge to dine formally with the children at least once weekly, and to instruct them on the language, placement, and use of table settings and all the trappings.

The Elite—even with its service-only-at-the-right-time policy— exceeded my expectations.

6

BYE BYE BLACKBIRD

Ettra and I spent an uneventful first night in the Admiral Semmes Hotel, disturbed only by the maid's early-morning knock.

Just minutes after I requested a later clean-up time, another knock summoned me to the door. There stood a handful of the maid's co-workers. They wanted to confirm with their own eyes her report of black guests in the hotel. I cordially acknowledged the prideful welcome on their gleeful faces.

When the Alabama Bar Association announced its annual meeting for 1964, I urged every black lawyer in the state to join me in Mobile. The main attraction for us would not be the hotel, the city, or the program.

Just about all of us watched or saw replays of the televised ceremony on July 2, 1964, as President Lyndon Baines Johnson—surrounded by Dr. King and the head of every major civil rights organization—signed into law the Civil Rights Act.

This landmark law banned racial discrimination in public accommodations. It represented the biggest gain ever in our legal struggle against segregation. I could think of no more fitting place to celebrate that achievement than the public hotel reserved for the Bar's annual weekend of educational and social activities. Perfect timing.

En route to the morning sessions, I encountered in the elevator the chief justice of the Alabama Supreme Court. "Seay," he responded to my greeting, "are you still trying to get all the nigras out of all the prisons?"

I understood his reference. I filed frequently, and with remarkable success, a record number of appellate petitions for wrongfully convicted prisoners. "If I had the resources, I could, Judge," came my quick rejoinder, "because they are all there illegally."

We parted ways, and I proceeded to the registration table. I requested two banquet tickets and presented ten dollars. "They are not available," the lawyer in charge politely intoned.

"You mean you have sold out already?"

When he repeated himself, I got the message.

"You mean they are not available to me?"

Clearly reluctant to recite the Bar Association's longstanding exclusion of black lawyers from social events, he replied, "My statement was 'they are not available.'"

I went outside to ponder my next move. An assistant U.S. attorney with whom I had sparred in the federal courthouse back in Montgomery spotted me sulking and pried from me the reason.

"Just give me your ten dollars, and I'll go get you some damn tickets," he responded immediately.

I seriously considered his offer before deciding not to involve him. Civil Rights Act notwithstanding, I knew it would take more than the tickets for Ettra and me to gain admission to this banquet. I also knew he would suffer holy hell for acting as my go-between for the tickets.

Instead of dressing for the banquet at the end of the day's business session, I took Ettra to dinner at the hotel's restaurant. Afterwards we sauntered over to the adjacent piano bar.

As soon as we seated ourselves at a table, the pianist stopped her tune in midstream and launched into a spirited rendition of "Bye Bye Blackbird."

When she finished, I calmly strode to the piano and placed a dollar in her tip cup. "That was just lovely," I affected my best Southern drawl. "Please play that again."

THE DRIVE BACK HOME to Montgomery seemed so much longer than the drive down to Mobile. Needless to say, our experience at the Admiral Semmes satiated my appetite for the Bar's annual meetings. I hardly glanced at the notices for either the 1965 meeting in Birmingham or the 1966 meeting in Huntsville.

Montgomery's turn as the host city came around again in 1967. For some reason, I lingered over the announcement and then handed Ettra this notice of scheduled activities for spouses:

PLEASE TAKE ME HOME TO YOUR WIFE.

FOR THE LADIES

Thursday, July 20, 1967

6:30–8:00 P.M. Reception, Blue & Gray Room, Whitley Hotel

Friday, July 21, 1967

11:30 A.M. sharp—Ladies will meet in the lobby of the Whitley Hotel. They will be transported by buses to the Country Club where cocktails and a luncheon will be served. After the luncheon the buses will take them for a tour of the Blount Home and Garden and the Thigpen Garden. This will be followed by a Tea at the Governor's Mansion.

7:30 P.M. Annual Banquet and Dance, Davis Room, Jefferson Davis Hotel

Dress: Ladies—Formal (Long or Short)

Men—Optional

There will be a special registration table set up for the ladies in the Whitley Lobby. Please come by this table as soon as convenient after your arrival in Montgomery. Please secure your complimentary luncheon ticket at the Registration Desk.

I registered for the meeting and persuaded William H. Thomas, a fellow alumnus of Howard Law School, to register. Thomas had been admitted to the Alabama Bar in 1967 and worked as a lawyer for the Veterans Administration. His wife, Barbara, decided to join my wife on the bus tour "for the ladies."

Still stinging from the Mobile fiasco, I phoned Harry Cole, the president that year of the Montgomery Bar Association: "Are all of the events associated with the annual meeting open and available to all registered members and their guests?"

When he responded without hesitation, "Sure," I quickly cautioned him to think about my question.

"Let me check with the organizers," he reflected, "and I will call you back."

To my surprise, he called within ten minutes and reaffirmed his report, with one potential exception—a formal dinner hosted by the First National Bank in honor of Robert E. Steiner, III, a bank officer who was the state Bar's outgoing president.

ETTRA HAD A SPECIAL request: Forty dollars for a fancy dress she'd eyed at A. Nachman's, the leading ladies' store in Montgomery. For me, in 1967, that was a big chunk of money for a dress. But why not, I reasoned, remembering Mobile.

So off Ettra went with my forty dollars and instructions to come back to the office before she headed to the bus tour. A fiercely proud black woman, Ettra did not suffer racism quietly. If the occasion demanded resistance, however, I wanted to temper her tongue this time and take the battle to court.

Ettra strutted back to the office in her new dress. She looked like a living doll.

"Just be cool," I cautioned. "When the bus gets to the Governor's Mansion, you will probably encounter a big guard at the gate, and he will be sporting a big gun; if he refuses to let you and Barbara onto the grounds, don't argue with him. Just ask him politely to call my office, tell me where you are, and have a state trooper escort you to my office."

From my office Ettra walked the three blocks to the Whitley Hotel. About fifteen minutes later she called to report that she and Barbara were not permitted even to get on the bus. She said that a man named Judge Scott[11] wanted to talk with me. My seething silence masked a serious "Black Attack." At least a minute passed before I told her to put him on the phone.

"Mr. Seay," he started with his apology, "I am so sorry this happened, but we had not made special arrangements for them." I declined his invitation for discussion.

My law partner at the time, Fred D. Gray, Sr., served along with me as local attorneys for the NAACP Legal Defense Fund. Headquartered then in New York, LDF had already gained stature as the best civil rights law firm in the country. An LDF lawyer just happened to be in our office that day. He, Fred, and every other lawyer in the office immediately stopped other case work and collaborated with me on the federal complaint I filed early the next morning, August 3, 1967:

Civil action no. 2589-N: Barbara Thomas, William Thomas, Ettra Seay, and Solomon S. Seay, Jr.; others similarly situated, v. Board of Commissioners of the State Bar of Alabama; James E. Clark, as President of the State Bar of Alabama; John B. Scott, individually and as Secretary of the Board of Commissioners and of the Alabama State Bar.

It took barely three months to end the lawsuit. In an affidavit by Scott, the bar acknowledged with regret the discriminatory rebuff to Barbara and Ettra—assigning it to an attempt to save them the embarrassment of being refused admittance at the Montgomery Country Club. He reported correctly his assurances that they would be welcomed at the annual banquet and, for future meetings, at any bar-sponsored social activity.

With the bar association's "on-the-record" agreement to open all sponsored events to all members, spouses, and guests, irrespective of race, we had achieved our primary goal. Thus we agreed to withdraw our claim for compensatory and punitive damages.

In hindsight, I should have held out for at least the forty dollars for Ettra's new dress.

About thirty-five years later, Ettra—still a fiercely proud black queen looking lovely in yet another new outfit—sat with me at another annual meeting, this time to witness Fred accept the gavel as the 126th president, and the first of color, of the Alabama State Bar Association.

7

The Color of Convenience

Halfway through my trial of a relatively minor case, Montgomery County Circuit Judge Eugene Carter declared a brief recess. Before heading back to the courtroom after leaving the restroom, I leaned down for a gulp of water at the fountain just steps away. Only afterwards did I glance upwards at the "whites only" sign. A deputy sheriff standing nearby caught my eye, and I beckoned him closer.

"I wonder what dumb son-of-a-bitch put the white water fountain right at the door to the colored men's toilet. Any colored man coming right out of this toilet is bound to stop right here for water, and you will be ready to jail him for breaking the law when he had no such intention."

"You know, Seay," the deputy pondered, "you asked a good question . . . that is kind of stupid, ain't it?"

He followed me back to the courtroom and strode right up to the bench where Judge Carter hovered over a host of lawyers mingling about for the trial docket.

"Judge," the deputy hollered as he pointed in my direction, "Lawyer Seay raised an interesting question in the hall a minute ago. He wondered what dumb son-of-a-bitch put the white water fountain right next to the door for the colored men's toilet."

Judge Carter didn't get rattled easily. "I did that," he replied. He proceeded to explain that he got tired of walking all the way to the other end of the hall for water at the fountain adjacent to the white men's toilet. So he had the fountain moved.

Not even for a minute did I believe that anyone actually moved that fountain. I would have bet my last buck that they simply switched the signs, and Judge Carter satisfied his thirst from the same stream of water previously reserved for only colored lips.

Quite mindful that the Judge now knew that I considered him a dumb son-of-a-bitch, I ordered my face not to portray my doubts. My client's fate stood in the balance, and to his credit, Judge Carter did not allow my brash inquiry to taint the outcome.

I did not hide my pleasure a few years later when my federal lawsuit banned Jim Crow from the county courthouse and thus allowed colored patrons of the courthouse the same convenience-driven choices as the Judge enjoyed.

Part Three

Liberty and Justice
For Those Who Got the Guts
To Grab It

"Evil prospers because good men fail to act."
— *African proverb (The Gambia)*

8

SAVING PEE WEE

I could have been born in Greenville, Alabama. Our family called it home in 1931. Daddy pastored an African Methodist Episcopal Zion church there and also ran the church-owned Lomax Hannon School.

For reasons never shared with me, my schoolteacher mother absolutely did not want me born anywhere in Butler County. After school on December 2, 1931, she managed the hour's drive, alone, to the Madison Park community a few miles north of Montgomery. Within minutes my maternal grandfather—the community's namesake, leader, and "midwife"—proudly delivered me, the first-born son of Carrie Madison and Solomon Snowden Seay, Sr.

As soon as she recovered, my mother wrapped me warmly and drove us back to Greenville. I spent my early childhood on the campus of my father's school.

Destiny delivered me back to Greenville about thirty years later, a grown-up lawyer on a "life or death" mission: to keep the state of Alabama from executing yet another hapless black boy.

The town still sported Butler County's signature camellias and magnolias. Cotton fields prospered. The fifties were coming to a close, but all the old ways had not yet gone with the wind. A handful of plantation farms still survived on the backs of poor blacks, and their owners thrived by controlling almost every aspect of the workers' lives.

Hardy heirs of plantation society's prime time encountered little resistance in their quest to perpetuate both the prerogatives and the profits of their ancestors. Plantation owners effectively controlled the quality of any education provided to the black workers' children; the crop seasons dictated the duration of not only each school day but also each school term.

The plantation owner served as the primary school administrator and exercised the authority delegated by law to the county board of education. Blacks were assigned as principals at these plantation schools but lacked any power to override the plantation owners' will.

One of these black principals educated me about "the way things are" on my first trip to investigate PeeWee's plight. The man absolutely bristled with joy as he shared cautious optimism that he would soon witness a first—a black student making it all the way through high school. "If [the plantation owner] will just let me keep the school open through the spring, we will make a full term, and the board of education will have to give him a diploma."

Small wonder that this desolate place in such bleak times nurtured a raging black man-child who leaned dangerously. His given name was Roosevelt Howard, but everyone called him PeeWee.

He toiled early, long, and every day on a plantation at the top of the "worst" list. The owner, Vandiver Lazenby, allowed no sharecropping. He cradled an abiding conviction that the good Lord created a whole race of people, PeeWee's people, for the primary purpose of picking his cotton.

Lazenby required all the laborers to buy food and other necessaries at his plantation store. And, of course, he kept all the records for their inevitable purchases on credit.

Mid-afternoon on January 9, 1960, PeeWee went to the plantation store for two dollars worth of sugar. Lazenby told him he did not have that much money on his account. The two argued, and PeeWee left the store.

According to the first-degree murder indictment, PeeWee "unlawfully, and with malice aforethought, killed Vandiver Lazenby by shooting him with a rifle." Witnesses saw PeeWee with a .22 rifle, headed in the direction of the store, where he posted himself at a back window and shot Lazenby in the back.[12]

A court-appointed white lawyer duly represented PeeWee before an all-white jury, with the predictable outcome on February 23, 1960: conviction and punishment fixed at death by electrocution.[13]

I first met PeeWee waiting to die at the old Kilby Prison only a stone's throw from my Madison Park home in north Montgomery. In late 1962 or early 1963 I started the cumbersome procedural maneuvers which eventually gave PeeWee a second and eventually a third chance at life.[14] Following his second trial in 1964 and another death sentence, the appellate proceedings kept me busy for almost seven years. When I finally secured a third trial, this time I signed on as PeeWee's trial counsel.

A MONTH OR SO before the third trial in January 1972, the circuit clerk interrupted my tedious review and hand-copying of records to tell me that Judge T. W. Thagard wanted to talk with me about PeeWee's case. I made my way inside his chambers.

I found the circuit solicitor who would prosecute PeeWee's case already comfortably settled in a corner chair. To my surprise, Judge Thagard stood up from behind his desk and cordially greeted me with an extended hand.

Not a very big man, the Judge spoke in a relatively quiet and calm voice. "Welcome home, Seay. I understand you were born in Greenville." When I corrected that report, he said, "Nevertheless, we're glad to have you here."

"Bub and I," he continued with a nod toward the circuit solicitor, "were talking about how, as far as we can remember, you are the first Negro attorney to appear in a case in the Circuit Court of Butler County, Alabama."

He assured me that I would be treated fairly. Our encounter ended with a sincerely intoned promise that I definitely welcomed: "Now, if you encounter any problems, you just let me know."

I thanked him just as sincerely and departed with a funny feeling that I might have reason to challenge his pledge of fairness sooner rather than later.

Like practically all state judicial buildings, Butler County's courthouse still strictly enforced segregation inside courtrooms and restrooms, and at water fountains. I launched my initial challenge to Judge Thagard's pledge of fairness: a motion to desegregate all spaces and facilities within the entire courthouse.

I made a strategic decision to limit the request to preliminary proceedings and the trial in PeeWee's case. Without requiring any evidence, and promptly after hearing my legal arguments, Judge Thagard granted the motion. He directed the sheriff to remove every race-specific sign posted throughout the courthouse. He also announced from the bench that spectators could choose to sit anywhere in the courtroom.

Though I understood that the signs of segregation would return after PeeWee's trial, I considered the temporary reprieve a huge victory for at least the appearance of justice. Notwithstanding his slight stature, the judge now stood ten feet tall in my view.

PeeWee's trial lasted several days. As if the *State of Alabama v. Pee-Wee Howard* did not present enough challenges for me, every lawyer in Butler County lined up with the prosecution and openly assisted with preliminary motions.

The courthouse filled a circle on the northern edge of town. In an abundance of precaution, I parked my car each day just beneath a window to the sheriff's first-floor office.

At the end of an afternoon proceeding I prepared for the drive home only to find both of my front tires slashed. I marched back inside and reported the incident to Judge Thagard. He made one phone call, and in short order someone towed my car to a local garage for new tires.

On the drive back to Montgomery, I scored the judge several notches taller.

But my troubles did not end.

Every evening for several days when I left the courthouse, I drove no more than two blocks before a motorcycle policeman pulled me over. His routine did not vary: he would ask for my driver's license, walk around my car, hand my license back to me, get on his motorcycle, and drive off without a word.

On the fourth day of yet another groundless stop, as I handed him my license, I snarled at him, "It is the same license I have had all week."

"Don't get smart with me, nigger," he retorted. He deliberately extended his swaggering circles around the car before tossing back my license and roaring away. The delay gave me just enough time to note his name on the silver badge fastened to his jacket.

I made an illegal U-turn without incident, drove back to the courthouse, and lodged my complaint with Judge Thagard. Again, he acted swiftly and decisively. I heard him order the Greenville police chief to bring the no-longer anonymous officer immediately to his chambers.

Within minutes I had the pleasure of witnessing an upright, fear-less, and honorable judge in a memorable profile of courage, atypical of elected judges in the racially turbulent times then sweeping the South. "Lawyer Seay has business with this court," Judge Thagard sternly advised the clearly daunted officers. "I am not going to tolerate any more harassment of him." Staring straight at the police chief, he promised contempt for him and time in the county jail for the harass-ing officer if I encountered any more problems with the Greenville Police Department.

As I left his chambers, the judge stood up, extended his hand and spoke sincerely, "Seay, I'm really sorry this happened, but I am sure it will not happen again."

I was not stopped again. Judge Thagard just seemed to grow taller and taller and taller.

THE CIRCUIT SOLICITOR STRUCK the few blacks on the venire, leaving an all-white jury for trial. I filed a panoply of pretrial motions and prevailed on none. Thus, I embraced with undiminished zeal the uphill obstacle course through trial.

To say that I felt jittery and apprehensive when the jury retired would be the understatement of the century. A young, relatively inexperienced black lawyer, trying to persuade an all-white jury to spare a young black man charged with the capital murder of one of the county's most well-known and well-off white men.

The unthinkable happened: the jury found PeeWee guilty but fixed his sentence at imprisonment for life.

The circuit solicitor could not hide his disappointment that Pee-

Wee would keep on breathing. The local lawyers who freely aided and applauded his cause seemed equally disgusted.

The outcome gratified and pleased me to no end. First and foremost, I saved PeeWee's life. Beyond that result—wholly unanticipated by any black person living in Butler County—I had witnessed two formidable triumphs of courage over fear in Alabama's Black Belt. First, a fair-minded and honorable white judge whose actions spoke as loudly as his words; next, a principled, all-white jury refusing to back down on an unpopular decision.

By the time I made it back to my Montgomery office, I felt not only that I, too, had grown a few feet taller but, if only for a moment, I believed I could fly!

9

Facing Fear

I came awfully close to death's door not long after I ventured into Chilton County wielding only my license to practice law. I have never been afraid to die. To die for nothing—that's a different ball game.

Sunday morning started innocently enough with a call from my brother-in-law, who operated his own funeral home in Clanton. Frequent client referrals from him kept me from starving as a young lawyer. His father owned a recreational spot on Mitchell Lake called Dixie's Camp and rented the lake cabins mainly to whites for fishing. The Wilson family was well-respected in Chilton County.

The Ku Klux Klan also enjoyed a respected place in the county. Members were plentiful, powerful, and persuasive. Especially when they traded their official daytime suits and uniforms for the notorious fright sheets prescribed for fiery nocturnal passions.

At the funeral home I gazed upon the remains of a grossly over-weight, dark-skinned man felled by three bullets to his chest. His untimely demise coincided with a Klan rally in Jemison, a few miles north of Clanton.

The KKK rally began on a Wednesday afternoon in November 1957, lasted until close to midnight, and kept the same schedule on Thursday, Friday, and Saturday. Uniformed state troopers, inside state cars parked alongside the road, kept watch from start to finish.

Most of the town's blacks lived on the side of a hill overlooking the rally camp. Preparing for the worst, the men dug perimeter fox holes and stocked in loaded shotguns and pistols. If the Klan started trouble, they would be ready, and the call for reserve support quickly brought more weapons and volunteers.

Just after dusk on Saturday the Klan came marching up the hill. The black community guessed it would be a Saturday night showdown, and their fortified trenches erupted in gunfire when the invaders made it to the halfway mark.

Down on the ground, troopers stopped a young black man driving in from a nearby town to join the resistance. Forced to abandon his car, he managed to escape and went running up the hill, dodging bullets. At the first house up the hill he pounded on the back door; unfortunately for him, it belonged to one of the few black men who refused to fight. His repeated knocks unanswered, the volunteer soldier hastened onward with troopers and hounds in hot pursuit.

The dogs stopped dead in their tracks at the same back door. Without warning, the troopers riddled the door with bullets. Three instantly killed the man now stretched out before me in the mortuary. Only the grace of God spared his wife and children—huddled with him inside the little house—from a similar fate.

On the hilly battlefield the Klan cavalry discovered right away that they were ill-suited for trench warfare. One tripped on his sheet and dropped his weapon as he fell; as he rolled over to retrieve it, he caught a shotgun blast in the arm. The emboldened black shooter ripped off the Klansman's hood and unmasked a longtime deputy sheriff.

Incredibly, despite all the shooting that rocked the hills in this Saturday night clash, death snared only the pitiful black man who never joined in the fight.

EVERY BLACK PERSON IN Chilton County expected trouble. Monday morning ushered in the first attack: Chilton County deputies rounded up a horde of black men in Jemison and arrested them for "assault with intent to murder."

At the circuit clerk's office I read the complaints and moved quickly to interview everyone in jail and get appearance bonds filed. Back to my "office" in the funeral home, I had barely sat down before a phone call from the spouse of one of the bonded men sent me rushing back to the jail. She had not heard from him.

No one at the jail could explain why everyone except this man had been released. I went straight to the sheriff's office.

A youthful-looking white woman at a reception desk listened but told me that I needed to talk directly with the sheriff. I gave her my phone number at the funeral home and requested that she ask the sheriff to call me when he returned to the office. She wrote down the number, recited it, and asked if she had it right.

"Yeah," I replied, "that's correct."

The scowl on her face matched the irritation in her voice. "You meant, 'Yes, ma'am'?"

I responded with my biggest and brightest smile, gave her a look, and walked out the door.

It did not take long for the sheriff's call. I started to give him the background on my jailed client, but he quickly interrupted and sounded mad as hell: "But I want to see you. Bring your ass back down to my office."

I declined my brother-in-law's offer to go with me. We agreed instead that he would trail me to the sheriff's office and watch me walk inside.

The "you-meant-yes-ma'am" woman was the first face I recognized.

Behind her desk I glimpsed a long table inside the sheriff's room. Three deputies not in uniform sat around the table, playing with batons and posturing with pistols; one pointed his carbine straight at me.

Standing in front of a closet door, at least six feet seven inches tall and three hundred pounds strong, the sheriff beckoned me inside and partially closed the door. At that moment the six by six space seemed to me only a little larger than the jail cell which held my client.

Shaking with anger, the sheriff hollered at me. "What the goddamn hell you mean insulting my wife?"

Young, cocky, and in pretty good shape at six feet four inches and a lean two hundred pounds, I would have taken him out easily in the first round back in my army boxing days. But we were far removed from that protected space. This was the sheriff and he had me trapped.

"Sir," I replied, not fully appreciating the situation, "I am afraid you got me mixed up with somebody else. I don't even know your wife."

"The hell you don't." He pulled the door further ajar and pointed to the woman at the reception desk. "That's my wife right there."

I knew then that I could not retreat. Not batting an eye, I kept my tone puzzled and plaintive. "Sheriff, I don't recall saying anything insulting to your wife. As a matter of fact, I would not intentionally insult any lady, black or white. That's just not my style. Now if I was so lax in my language that your wife misinterpreted something that I said and thought it was insulting, then perhaps I owe her an apology."

Unmoved, the sheriff got right in my face and ended a furious, profanity-laced tirade with a promise I did not take as an empty threat.

"Seay, I will put my foot so far up your ass, you will spit it out your mouth. You come up here all the time, and that's all right, because the niggers up here need somebody to help them. And you can keep on coming up here. And if you keep your goddamn nose clean, and don't act like a goddamn fool, me and you will git along almost as if you was a white man."

I struggled to keep my mouth shut and my hands down. For the first time in my life, I felt real fear. Death did not scare me. I just did not want to die in Chilton County for not saying "Yes, ma'am" to a white woman—it seemed to me that Sol Seay deserved a better reason for dying.

Fewer than ten black lawyers practiced in the entire state of Alabama at the time. Along with Fred Gray and Orzell Billingsley, I stayed busy in Chilton County for months before we succeeded in getting every single case dropped. I also managed not to take on the sheriff.

IO

A PROMISE KEPT

About forty robed Klansmen paid a broad-daylight visit to the carnival shortly after it staked a site near the Chilton County airport. They headed straight for the booth where a black woman was said to be "out of her place . . . acting like she owned the stand."

The lady traveled with a street-corner carnival parading the usual mix of animal and freak shows, rides, games, and food. She operated a concession stand, and the only other black person in the crew worked as a handy man.

Just one look at the white wave moving toward her, and she took off running. She left behind not only her wares but also the storage trailer which doubled as her home during the carnival's run. Someone directed her to my office for help in getting back her trailer, if not her livelihood.

I had my doubts. As I processed the details of her harrowing encounter, I remembered my own bout with the Chilton County sheriff.

Sometimes all the courage tank needs is a good infusion of cash. I politely averted my eyes from her buxom front as she retrieved a bundle of bills to cover my retainer fee. I then made my way to Clanton and plotted my strategy all the way.

At my brother-in-law's funeral home I detached a trailer from his pickup truck, and drove the truck straight to the sheriff's office.

He betrayed no emotion as I described the suspects responsible for my client's plight: "About forty white men wearing white sheets with pillowcases over their heads." (One never referred to the Klan by name in conversation with white folks.)

I then displayed the signed pick-up authorization I had prepared for my client. Humbly, I asked the sheriff to escort me out to the carnival and to stay while I secured her trailer.

"Seay," the sheriff responded, "go on out there and git it."

"No, sir, I want you to go with me." Though I knew he understood well the reason for my request, I solemnly sounded the fear which signaled a victory for him: "The same men wearing those sheets and pillowcases will probably run me off. That's why I want you with me."

No doubt relishing the apprehension I effected so unsuspectingly, the sheriff repeated, "Seay, ain't nobody going to bother you; go on out there and git the trailer."

I had to play my trump card then.

"Sheriff," I now sounded both surprised and scared, "you remember one of the last things you said to me when I came to your office about two months ago? You told me I could keep on coming up here, and if I kept my goddamn nose clean and didn't act like a goddamn fool, me and you would get along almost as if I was a white man. Well, I remembered that and took it to heart, and now I need you to go with me to get that trailer."

"Hell, Seay, come on." Clearly annoyed, the sheriff bounded from his chair. I confidently followed him to the carnival grounds, hooked up my client's trailer, and basked in the security of the sheriff's escort all the way to the Montgomery County line.

When I pulled up to my law office and delivered to my client her trailer home—along with a fistful of my business cards—I felt mighty proud of myself. The magnificent smile on her lovely black face made my day.

The good feeling lingered as I considered the sheriff's promise to treat me "almost as if I was a white man . . . if I didn't act like a goddamn fool." I'm sure he felt he taught me a lesson.

I chuckled, wondering just how long it would take the sheriff to unravel the lesson I had just practiced on him: Never make promises that you don't intend to keep.

11

I Cried Real Tears

W hat in the hell happened in there?" I could not mask my boiling anger when I cornered the young black foreman who had read the jury's verdict.

"Lawyer Seay, we got all mixed up the third time the judge sent us back, and that little old white lady who was sitting on the front row just took over."

She and the only other white person on the jury believed from the beginning in my client's guilt. The ten blacks—all serving as jurors for the first time—thought the evidence showed more than the reasonable doubt I argued.

"'Y'all just don't understand the jury system yet,' she told us. 'I've been here so many times I can't count them. I know the judge. He's told us three times now that our verdict must be unanimous, and that means he plans to keep us here until we agree on a guilty verdict.' That's when we decided to go along with her, Lawyer Seay. We just didn't know any better."

I shuffled away from him without another word. Inside my car, there in the parking lot of the Lowndes County courthouse, I cried. I shed real, man-size tears.

The crushing verdict came in my first case tried to a Lowndes County jury which finally looked more like me and my black defendant than the prosecutor and the judge. The transformation had been a long time coming through years of lawsuits.

Blacks had been excluded routinely from jury service in most state courts, particularly in the Black Belt counties. Black civil litigants opposing whites harbored no hope for success. Black criminal defendants expected not only guilty verdicts but also harsher sentences at the hand of juries which then had authority for both decisions.

We tackled the problem first on a case-by-case basis. In just about every criminal case, I filed challenges to the racial composition of every component in the jury selection process, from the box of registered voters or property owners from whom potential jurors were selected to the predictably all-white trial jury. My partner, Fred Gray, followed the same pattern in his civil cases. Our invariable failures prompted a new strategy: federal court lawsuits against the jury commissioners in targeted Black Belt counties—including Lowndes County—to enjoin the systematic exclusion of blacks from jury service. It worked![15]

I went to Lowndes County to defend a black farmer charged with possession and distribution of marijuana. Acting on a tip from an unidentified informant, and without benefit of a search warrant, state agents went out to his farm, raked up some loose hay in his barn, and found what they identified as some leaves from marijuana plants.

This time the available jury pool pretty much reflected the nearly 90 percent black population of Lowndes County. Still, I could not use my limited number of "strikes" to secure an all-black jury. But if I could have, believe me, I would have. The jury had ten blacks and two whites, and I was comfortable with that makeup.

The trial judge denied all my pretrial motions attacking the search, the "chain of custody" for the evidence, and technical deficiencies in the indictment. At trial, I focused on the lack of evidence to support any charge of distribution, the lack of evidence for specific intent, and the minuscule amount of marijuana found, if any.

It was not a long or difficult trial.

After about two hours, the jury returned to announce its verdict. I was absolutely certain, given all facts and circumstances, that the verdict would be not guilty.

My confidence increased when the tall young black man stood to identify himself as the selected foreman. "Has the jury reached a verdict?" the judge inquired.

"Well . . . yes." I quickly noted the foreman's hesitation.

"What is your verdict?"

"Well . . . guilty."

The foreman sounded much too reticent, and I promptly requested that the jury be polled to determine if all agreed.

"Is this your verdict?" Starting with the first row, the judge repeated the question to each juror. The third juror, a young black woman, responded loudly, "No, sir, I ain't never thought he was guilty."

Immediately I jumped up and started screaming for a mistrial. The judge directed me to sit down until he completed the polling. I was glad that he stopped me because three other blacks on that jury declared that they did not agree with the guilty verdict.

Again, the judge denied my motion for mistrial. Instead, he recharged the jury on the "law of the case" and sent them back into the jury room for further deliberations.

Another two hours lapsed; after determining that the jury's knock signaled a verdict, the judge had the jurors ushered back into the jury box.

The foreman reported another "guilty" verdict, but I sensed again his initial hesitation. I demanded a poll of the jury.

This time around a fifth juror joined those who remained steadfast in their declared belief in the defendant's innocence.

Refusing my renewed motion for mistrial, the judge gave the jurors another charge on the law and admonished them that their verdict had to be unanimous. Back to the jury room.

After no more than thirty minutes, the jury returned, and the foreman announced, for the third time, a guilty verdict. This time each juror affirmed the verdict.

The sentence followed without any deliberations: a prison term of ten years. After giving oral notice of appeal, I tried to comfort my flabbergasted client before I confronted the foreman.

His report bothered me for more than a little while. Had all of our work in getting blacks on juries been in vain? Or, had I simply failed to question and assess these jurors correctly during the selection process? What could I have asked to be certain that they fully understood their individual responsibilities to reach independent judgements on guilt or innocence?

The judge's curt denials of my mistrial motions left me with no hope of success with a motion for a new trial based on the jury's confusion. An immediate appeal seemed more promising. In the first place, at that time Alabama boasted a rather progressive Court of Criminal Appeals, if you could get there. Additionally, the appellate rules required the judges to search the entire record for error, and a conviction could be reversed for reasons not presented by the defendant on appeal.

Getting a case heard by the Court of Criminal Appeals, however, presented a procedural obstacle course of the worst kind. The record had to be on manuscript paper, tied in a specified manner by ribbon of a specific color. A statute dictated mandatory language for the trial court's certification of the record. Common-law rules of pleading and procedure ruled the day. The Alabama legislature resisted frequent attempts to align Alabama with the *Federal Rules of Civil and Criminal Procedure*. The majority didn't mind publicizing their fears: all the civil rights lawyers in the state worked for the NAACP, and the NAACP lawyers were taught and skilled in federal procedures.

Shortly after I filed the appeal I received a "Certificate of Affirmance and Dismissal of the Appeal." The stated ground: "Certificate of the Clerk—Improper."

Absolutely dumbfounded, I decided after an hour or so to throw myself on the mercy of Miss Mollie Jordan, the most venerable and kind-hearted clerk who ever graced the Alabama Court of Criminal Appeals. A fantastic lady simply called "Miss Mollie," she often visited the prisons—on her own time, on weekends—and went inside the cell blocks to talk with prisoners about their appeals. She explained rulings and procedures for securing from her office various records needed for their appeals. Practically every inmate in the Alabama prison system at that time knew, or had heard of, Miss Mollie Jordan and her reputation for fairness and concern.

Miss Mollie seemed to be waiting just for me as soon as I walked into the door. "Mr. Seay, you are late. I expected you over an hour ago." After assuring me that "lawyers much older and with much more experience have fallen into this same trap," she patiently instructed me on the forms and pleadings I needed to file, the corrected certificate to be signed by the clerk, and the proper binding method for the record on appeal.

I followed precisely Miss Mollie's road map to revive my appeal. When I filed all the necessary documents with a motion to withdraw the certificate of affirmance, I whispered thanks to the good Lord for Miss Mollie.

In less than a week, the Court of Criminal Appeals entered an order withdrawing its certificate of affirmance and remanding the case to the circuit court of Lowndes County, with instructions to dismiss the prosecution with prejudice.

Eventually the state repealed its arcane procedures and adopted substantially the *Federal Rules of Civil and Criminal Procedure*. But for Miss Mollie, though, my client would have languished a long time in prison.

12

A WIDOW'S MIGHT

The old widow squirreled away hard-earned dollars year in and year out before she could buy the first house. Then came the second and the third, and in short order she owned half a dozen little houses decent enough to rent. Now here come the people from the City talking about taking every single one of them for some kind of development.

"Lawyer Seay, what they talkin' 'bout givin' me is just a sin and a shame. And looks like they plannin' to tear up our whole community for this."

For the most part, Alabama built freeways and urban development projects by tearing down or through thriving black communities. What the city fathers planned for Opelika, I had witnessed already in scores of cities across east and central Alabama. In virtually every case, the city paid paltry sums as "just compensation" for the properties taken.

The Opelika Housing Authority sent an agent to this widow's home to offer $9,000 for her houses. He left in a hurry when she countered with a promise of $9,000 worth of buckshot in his butt if he did not get off her property. Believe you me, she meant it.

The housing authority then sent a housing inspector to post "condemned" signs on each of the houses. That's when she sent for me.

In Opelika I called first on the housing inspector and demanded a complete list of every deficiency at each house. A rather decent fellow, he readily admitted that he had not inspected any of the houses. He simply responded to the housing authority's request. Nothing at any of the houses warranted a condemnation notice. After he removed every single notice, he even apologized personally to my client.

The housing authority forged ahead with a backup plan: filing a condemnation petition in the county probate court.

I seized the offense with a plethora of pleadings which challenged an issue rarely contested, the city's power to condemn. I asserted every conceivable constitutional claim, common-law remedy, and statutory defense.

An unprecedented week-long trial focused only on the city's authority to condemn private property. As expected, on this issue the probate court sided with the housing authority. I achieved my purpose—to blow as much smoke as possible and maximize publicity for a race-based claim.

The issue shifted to "just compensation." The probate judge appointed a three-person commission for the trial which lasted three full days and half of another. Predictably again, the commissioners set an award which, by any reasonable standard, amounted to theft of my client's property.

On with an appeal to the circuit court of Lee County and a jury trial. Though I knew the probabilities favored an all-white jury, I made a conscious decision to make race the issue at trial. I gambled that substantial evidence of the city's callous mistreatment of this old black widow would infuriate even white jurors. It did.

The jury returned precisely the verdict I requested. After deducting attorney's fees and expenses, I delivered the widow a check in excess of $100,000, drawn from our law firm's trust account.

Over a year later the firm's banker called me to confirm my signature on the check. As he described the lady who wanted to have the proceeds transferred to another bank, I almost fell out of my chair. He agreed to make her comfortable while I rushed down to the bank.

I had to find out why the widow sat on that check for so long. Her response flabbergasted me: she had no immediate need for the money!

That sweet old lady's bulldog tenacity inspired my hardest work ever on a condemnation case, and all the time I thought she would be destitute without her rental properties. I wanted to tell her that the fees I owed to her victory came just in time for my family to enjoy a merry, merry Christmas!

13

FOOLS PROFIT
FROM THEIR OWN MISTAKES

Y ou are in touch with WVAS, the voice of Alabama State University. It's the first day of August 2001. Stay tuned for the news at the top of the hour."

The radio is my constant companion on the highway, and as the disc jockeys love to say, it "stays locked" on 90.7–FM, the Montgomery public radio station with a jazz format.

Today I am driving from Madison Park to Lake Jordan for a peek at the builder's progress on the steps designed to ease my increasingly difficult walk from our boat house up the hill to our lake house.

The feature story on the news grabs my attention: a veteran state trooper is fired for not meeting his quota of traffic citations. Official policy required the trooper to make a minimum of five contacts with civilian motorists daily, and at least two stops must result in citations. According to the news report, Alabama demanded strict compliance with the policy as a condition of the trooper's continued employment.

Immediately my memory raced back thirty-five years to a young John Hulett. After working outside the state for many years, Hulett returned to live in his native Lowndes County and care for his ailing father. His "reckless driving" arrest on October 1, 1965, triggered our "attorney-client" relationship.

With assistance from the NAACP's Legal Defense Fund, I sued in federal court to enjoin Hulett's scheduled trial before a justice of the peace in Lowndes County. Because the state compensated justices of the peace (who usually had no legal training) based solely on fines collected from the traffic violators they convicted, I argued that their direct, personal, and substantial interest in the prosecutions deprived defendant motorists of "due process of the law." A three-judge court readily agreed with my constitutional claim, temporarily restrained proceedings before the justice of the peace, and following trial, issued a permanent injunction.[16]

As I recalled this decision—which led to the demise of justices of the peace in Alabama—I simply could not believe the broadcast report. How could the state, I wondered, rationalize any constitutional distinction between forcing state troopers to ticket a minimum number of motorists or forfeit their jobs and compensating justices of the peace only if they convicted the cited motorists and the state collected the imposed fines?

"A fool profits from his own mistakes; wise men profit from the mistakes of others." I cannot attribute this wisdom to its original source—my European history professor did when I first heard it in a college classroom—but I concur wholeheartedly. On the subject of civil rights and constitutional liberties, history rightfully casts Alabama with the slow learners.

After John Hulett thwarted his unconstitutional trial before a justice of the peace, suddenly he found himself thrust into the Lowndes County leadership of the nascent movement to secure voting rights for black Alabamians. With assistance from Student Non-Violent Coordinating Committee (SNCC) activists Stokely Carmichael, George Green, and Bob Mantz, Hulett joined the Jackson family of White Hall, among others, in establishing the Lowndes County Freedom Organization, which promoted massive voter registration campaigns. He became the organization's first director.

The movement to register blacks as voters encountered incredible hostility in Lowndes County. Intimidation in every form imaginable came from official and private sources, but determined bands of black men and women continued to register in unbelievable numbers. John Hulett signed in first, becoming the first black registered voter in Lowndes County since Reconstruction.

Hulett rose to be the first black sheriff elected in the county and enjoyed a lengthy tenure before assuming another elected first as the county's probate judge. One of the most respected public servants in the entire state, John spent his retirement years quietly clearing the Lowndes County highways and byways of littered cans, recycling them, and setting aside the sales proceeds for a scholarship fund he used to help countless high school graduates make it through college.

The Lowndes County Freedom Organization co-founded by Hulett remained a strong presence for years after its successful voter registration campaigns. It registered as a political party and offered candidates in a number of local races. The symbol adopted by this new political party—a Black Panther—paid homage to the tireless leadership of Bob Mantz in sustaining the organization from its voter registration campaigns through its development as a political party. Stokely Carmichael often said that Mantz—a tall, wiry, very dark-complexioned, and physically imposing man—reminded him of a black panther, and he gave him that nickname. It stuck with him . . . and with the Black Panther party born and bred in Lowndes County, Alabama.

PART FOUR

FEARLESS FREEDOM FIGHTERS

"Power concedes nothing without a demand."

— Frederick Douglass

14

THE TURKEY BONE WARRIORS

D addy Bone wore his moniker as proudly as he wrapped his neck every day with a huge turkey bone, polished and dangling from a leather strap. When the going got tough and the white folks started acting ugly, he licked on that bone to control his anger.

It worked for him. Of all the Student Non-Violent Coordinating Committee (SNCC) leaders I met during their civil rights campaigns in Alabama, Daddy Bone ranked near the top on my short list of the truly nonviolent.

SNCC chose him to organize the movement in Eufaula, a sleepy little town nestled on the banks of the Chattahoochee River, about ninety miles southeast of Montgomery. The crappie fishing capital of the world as well as the largest town in Barbour County, Eufaula is not the county seat. That distinction belongs to Clayton, home of Alabama's most famous (or infamous, depending on your perspective) native son, Governor George Corley Wallace.

The turkey bone came to symbolize the freedom movement in Eufaula, and with Daddy Bone in firm command, the voting registration drives and business boycotts that kicked off the year in 1966 succeeded without violence.

SNCC supporters across the South traveled to join the local

masses. Each day ushered in fresh waves of peaceful demonstrations and pickets of selected downtown businesses which did not hire blacks in meaningful numbers or positions. For the most part, blacks, and even some whites, respected the boycott.

City leaders, prodded by bottom-line-conscious merchants, soon reached their breaking point. The city council enacted an anti-picketing ordinance which criminalized picketing without a permit while vesting in the mayor sole discretion to issue a permit. Applications for picketing permits had to be filed six days in advance. The ordinance limited the number of picketers authorized for a single permit and specified their spacing during a picket.

Eufaula police immediately launched mass arrests of protestors for picketing without permits and otherwise violating the hastily enacted ordinance. Daddy Bone called for Lawyer Seay.

Initially I made the nearly two-hour drive from Montgomery daily. As the cycle of pickets and arrests mounted, I decided to stay in Eufaula for a day or so. At the end of a grueling day alternating between jail interviews and courtroom appearances, I stopped for toiletries at one of the few stores not being boycotted. I left there in search of a pint of warmth to offset my anticipated boredom in a small hotel with limited amenities.

Surprise and dismay! SNCC had extended the boycott to the only liquor store in town. I could only wish they had waited at least another day for I was neither foolish nor courageous enough to drive across the river into Georgia.

When I arrived at the hotel, I promptly telephoned Mayor Hamp Graves and related my plight. A very personable fellow—not really distinguished as a lawyer—the mayor never struck me as a racist. "My bar is stocked, Seay, come on over to my house." I could hear him still laughing as I hung up the phone. Within minutes we were seated at his kitchen table—drinking some oddly named, overly sweet liqueur—and calling each other dirty names. The night passed quickly.

Eufaula hired Ira DeMent, an exceptionally able attorney who later rose to prominence first as U.S. attorney and then as U.S. district judge in the Montgomery federal courthouse which became my second home. Unfortunately for him, at that time he happened to be on the wrong side of the law. I consistently rapped his knuckles.

All the arrested demonstrators were tried and convicted in the city recorder's court. The city jail could not hold them all, and the overflow went to the Barbour County jail in Clayton. Among them was a young white girl, the daughter of an Air Force general; her status, race, youth, and gender all factored to make her a particular object of police officers' wrath.

State law then gave anyone convicted in the recorder's court only seven days to perfect an appeal to the county circuit court. The massive arrests created two strategic problems for me. First, many of the youths jailed, like the general's daughter, resided outside Alabama, making it problematic to get appearance bonds and file timely appeals. Second, the circuit judge for Barbour County was none other than Gerald Wallace, brother of Governor George.

On the seventh day—at or about the seventh hour—I rented a Twin Comanche with an instrument-rated pilot, picked up a bail bondsman, and flew to Clayton in "below minimums" weather.

For the fifteen or twenty persons jailed in Clayton, the sheriff, previously unknown to me, immediately made it clear that he had no intention of wasting his time completing the necessary "jail identification" cards. I proceeded to fill in the statistical data requested: name, race, date of birth, height, weight, residence, occupation. To expedite the process, I penned a big "C" by race on every card, without respect to the person.

I watched the sheriff thumbing through the stack of completed cards and suspected he was looking for the young white girl's card. "Sue is white," he declared after scrutinizing her card; "What is this 'C' for?" I casually replied, "Caucasian."

The sheriff again fumbled through the stack until he retrieved Daddy Bone's. Darting his eyes repeatedly from the card to me, he inched closer toward me and snarled: "Daddy Bone is a nigra. How come you got 'C' on his card?"

"Sheriff," I maintained my casual tone, "that stands for Colored."

I realized that I had just destroyed the possibility of an amicable relationship with the sheriff. He spared my clients the consequences I expected on the next round. His face could not mask his tremendous relief in getting all of the demonstrators out of his jail. From the time of their arrests to my appearance to secure their releases, they had treated the jail as just another place to rally—continuously singing freedom songs, yelling freedom slogans, and enthusiastically attempting to enlist inmates to join the movement once released.

After arranging for the bonded demonstrators either to get back home or to secure reasonably comfortable lodging for the night, I collapsed in the plane for our departure from the little country air strip to Montgomery's airport. It was one hell of a ride.

The "below-minimums" weather had deteriorated substantially. The elderly bondsman had no prior experience flying in a small propeller-driven aircraft, and it showed. When the plane dropped about thirty or forty feet, he reached up as if to grab onto something overhead; instinctively, I laughed and joked that if he fell, anything he grabbed would surely fall with him. He did not appreciate my humor, cursed me in colorful profanity, and vowed that he would never again accompany me anywhere to sign any bonds for any of my people.

As we hovered above the Montgomery Airport, then called Dannelly Field, the tower controller shouted to the pilot, "What the hell are you still doing up there?" He managed to keep an approaching Delta Airlines pilot on hold and cleared us to land. As we descended to about five hundred feet, the weather seemed to clear miraculously, and we enjoyed an unexpectedly smooth landing.

Within a week I filed petitions for removal to federal court of all the released protestors with appeals pending in the Barbour County circuit court as well as arrested protestors awaiting trials in the recorder's court. The petitions named all the demonstrators arrested on January 15, 16, 17, and 19. At the conclusion of the consolidated hearing on February 23, 1966, U.S. District Judge Frank M. Johnson, Jr., granted the removal petition pursuant to Findings and Conclusions announced from the bench.

Based on "practically uncontroverted evidence," Judge Johnson found that the January 15 protestors were not "disorderly" and, at the time of their arrest and immediately prior thereto, engaged in exercising a "constitutionally permissible right." Arresting them for non-compliance with the anti-picketing ordinance "was a denial of their equal protection under the law":

> The court finds that their arrest under this ordinance, under chief Abbott's testimony—and it is uncontroverted—was just a guise, nothing more than a subterfuge; that the Chief testified that 'We'—and I take it he was speaking for the City officials—decided to do something about the economic boycott, because the boycott had

become so effective, the situation among the merchants had become quite tense. The court finds from Chief Abbott's testimony—and it is also not controverted on this point—that the real reason for the arrest of these individuals on the 15th, and these in the other cases on the 16th, 17th, and 19th, was that the economic boycott had become effective, and that pressure had been put on the City authorities, and the City authorities, including the Chief of Police, decided that it was absolutely necessary to do something about it. That is the reasonable inference to draw from the testimony, and the court draws that inference.[17]

Judge Johnson cited three constitutional defects in the ordinance:

> Unconstitutional, in the first place, because it vests too much discretion in the Mayor—the issuing authority. Unconstitutional, in the second place, because it constitutes an undue prior restraint on anyone who desires to exercise their rights that might involve a public assembly, within the meaning of this particular Ordinance, and as "Public Assembly" is defined. The court also finds it is unconstitutional because it requires a permit, a laying over for a period of six days, and discretion vested in the Mayor as to whether he issues it then or not, if even two or more persons want to meet together for any of the purposes stated in the Ordinance.[18]

By formal order filed February 25, 1966, the court declared Eufaula's anti-picketing ordinance unconstitutional on its face and in its application to the arrested protestors, and he enjoined all the criminal prosecutions.[19]

15

Cottonreader
and the Chinaberry Tree

I last saw a chinaberry tree shading a house at the top of the hill on Perdue street in Greenville, Alabama. The year was 1965.

Too early for autumn's golden yellow foliage, it was still a beautiful ornamental with its glossy, dark green leaves. Once much more common along Alabama's roadsides, the umbrella-shaped tree has stout twigs which are greenish-brown; springtime blooms yield fragrant white petals, and a yellow berry-like fruit sprouts throughout the winter.

Almost as striking as the chinaberry tree was the amazing sight I witnessed a month or so earlier from my perch high on the steps of the historic Alabama Supreme Court building in downtown Montgomery.

A rowdy crowd of youthful demonstrators gathered on Dexter Avenue for a voting rights rally near the state capitol. Uniformed police officers—facing outward with sidearms and batons in ready position—encircled them completely. Marchers could exit but the officers did not allow anyone to penetrate the perimeter.

Not an uncommon sight in the 1960s, the demonstrators, many

not yet old enough to vote, carried home-made placards: "Freedom Now!" "Voting is a Right!" "Fired UP!" They had been organized by the Southern Christian Leadership Conference (SCLC).

Their leader, R. B. Cottonreader, provided the not-so-common antics which kept me riveted.

He had left the circle of demonstrators ostensibly for a restroom break. When he attempted to rejoin the demonstrators, a police officer repelled him with an upraised baton stretched between his hands. Cottonreader responded with the agility of a cocky defensive tackle primed to sack the quarterback: he took a few steps back, crouched his five-foot-seven, 150-pound frame into a running stance, and charged the police line. Again, an outstretched baton blocked his path.

The scene replayed a number of times. Predictably, Cottonreader did not prevail. I marveled at the officers' restraint, fully expecting one to bring the circus to a swift end with a body-blow swing of his baton. Where in the world did the SCLC find this man?

Cottonreader claimed to be from Chicago, but I later learned he'd taken a train from Mississippi. He called himself SCLC's County Project Director. From what I witnessed that day, his leadership style needed to be the first project.

Not long after the demonstration ended, Cottonreader showed up in my office. That face-to-face encounter, during which he described his "mission" in Alabama, convinced me that Cottonreader modeled himself more after Stokely Carmichael than Martin Luther King.

It would be several weeks before our next interaction. A black minister in Greenville phoned late one night for my insight on "a civil rights worker named R. B. Cottonreader." It seems Cottonreader had organized regular demonstrations around the Butler County courthouse to protest the abysmally few number of blacks allowed on the voter registration rolls.

None of the area ministers had joined the protest or offered their churches for mass meetings. So the protesters congregated for their rallies and marches in front of a large chinaberry tree in the front yard of a local activist who lived on Perdue Street.

The reverend hastened to assure me that the ministerial community embraced the goal of the protests. Butler County had more than a 40 percent black population but registered voters included barely 10 percent of the age-eligible blacks.[20]

"Lawyer Seay," he explained, "this man Cottonreader acts crazy for somebody with the SCLC, and he is making it hard for us to follow him."

Cottonreader began escorting marchers from the chinaberry tree to the courthouse in June 1965, and his campaigns continued aggressively through the year.

Initially the marchers, usually fewer than two hundred, stayed true to the principles of peaceful protest and passive resistance. Law enforcement officers soon showed less and less interest in protecting the marchers from increasingly hostile and frequently armed gangs of white bystanders. City officials arbitrarily denied march permits.

With or without permits, and frequently without even applying for one, Cottonreader led almost-daily marches from the chinaberry tree. If stopped by city officials declaring the march "an unlawful assembly," the demonstrators sat down in the street and sang protest songs.

Confrontations between marchers and angry whites inevitably turned physical. Officers tear-gassed marchers who ignored orders to disperse and often looked away as white antagonists joined the fray with billy clubs.

After achieving measurable progress in the voter registration campaign,[21] Cottonreader expanded the protests by mid-August to peaceful pickets in front of downtown Greenville stores that had no black employees. Decidedly more orderly than the voting rights demonstrators, the picketers marched in a single-file line designed not to interfere with customer traffic. Law enforcement officers kept watch but refused to restrain a crowd of taunting whites. One picketer suffered a severe kicking and beating by three whites who were never arrested.

When the picketers retreated to the top of the hill on Perdue Street, they discovered the ultimate insult to their injuries: gone was their beloved chinaberry tree, hacked down and hauled away by the City of Greenville.

LOSING THE SYMBOLIC CENTER of their movement seemed to empower Cottonreader and his followers to abandon an already shaky commitment to the law-abiding activism envisioned by SCLC's founders. "By any means necessary" became the inspirational slogan—in fact if not voiced—for the protests which followed.

Marches now proceeded without permits at nighttime or deliberately at the height of daytime traffic. Cottonreader boldly ventured inside the all-black Butler County Training School in a disruptive attempt to recruit demonstrators; the interference caused officials to close down the school more than once.[22]

City officials retaliated by steadfastly ignoring demonstrators' requests for protection and by allowing white thugs to brandish knives and guns as marchers passed by. Officials continued to deny even narrowly tailored permits for daytime protests and recklessly deployed tear gas and smoke bombs to disperse protesters.

In response to our federal lawsuit for an injunction to ensure safety for the demonstrators, the mayor, police chief, and sheriff filed a counterclaim demanding a stop to protests which obstructed traffic and school operations. For the "explosive situation" which worsened between June and November, Judge Frank M. Johnson, Jr., chastised all parties. "The fault lies on both sides," he declared in an opinion setting injunctions for everyone's conduct.[23]

While I took exception to some aspects of the injunction against the protesters, my "by any means necessary" clients should not have expected to be rewarded for their outrageous tactics. When the court taxed costs equally against plaintiffs and defendants, however, I had a hard time explaining why the total did not include their beloved chinaberry tree!

16

BERT & DAN . . .
AND THE KU KLUX KLAN

The middle-aged white woman sitting on a suitcase at the front door of my law office could not have been more conspicuous: she sported a "soul sister" beret, a "free Cuba" lapel pin, and a raised-fist "Black Power" emblem adorned her blue blazer.

"Mr. Seay," she rose and extended her hand as if I expected her, "I'm ready to go to work."

The year since our initial contact had not dimmed my memory of Bertha Nussbaum. Then—on the last day of the 1965 Selma to Montgomery March—and there—in the black-owned Pick's Restaurant in downtown Montgomery—she stood out in the lunchtime crowd.

Pulling over a chair right next to mine, she introduced herself and confidently declared her mission to be a civil rights attorney "down South." A Jewish divorcee in the third year of law school at the University of Washington, she had relinquished to her husband custody of their children in order to pursue a legal career. I handed her my card as I hurried out and told her to look me up after law school; I did not expect to see her again.

BERTHA'S PASSION FOR CIVIL rights plus undeniable legal skills readily secured her entry into our law firm when she reappeared after law school. Already admitted to the federal bar, she soon became my valued "associate counsel" in countless lawsuits filed for school desegregation, public accommodations, criminal justice, and voting rights.

Bert, as we called her, had two habits which proved only disruptive but a third fell in the dangerous category.

She tended to work odd hours, oftentimes all night and sometimes not at all during office hours. This habit predictably generated a fair amount of resentment from the female secretaries. Because she always completed her assignments on time, and with uniformly exceptional quality, I easily resolved the controversy in Bert's favor.

Bert's accustomed participation in protest demonstrations presented more of a dilemma.

Our official policy discouraged any such involvement by attorneys and staff for a very practical reason: arrests were increasingly inevitable, and we were on call "24-7" to gain the expeditious release of incarcerated protestors and otherwise represent them in court. Having our own employees arrested depleted our limited resources and diverted our necessary focus. After I had to pull Bert out of picket lines at city hall and at the state capitol on more than one occasion, she finally got the message and curtailed her marching.

Everything then moved along rather smoothly . . . until a massive campaign of voting rights protests got underway in neighboring Autauga County, and unmasked Bert's dangerous habit.

Assisted by the Student Non-Violent Coordinating Committee, the Autauga County Voters Association and the Autauga County Improvement Association organized the demonstrations. Dan Houser, a black resident of Prattville, led both associations.

I would have had to be utterly blind not to notice Bert's affection for Dan. Apparently their "social" relationship did not escape the attention of Prattville law enforcement.

The day of reckoning unraveled in Prattville on Sunday, June 11, 1967.

Between seventy-five and one hundred demonstrators gathered in the yard of the First Baptist Church, across the street from the Autauga County Improvement Association office, for a scheduled 3 P.M. meeting. When SNCC's Stokely Carmichael began his speech, his fiery rhetoric soon triggered a heated exchange with Prattville police officer Kenneth "Kennedy" Hill, who, months earlier, had shot in the back a black man attempting to escape from the Autauga County Courthouse.[24]

Carmichael: [Speaking to crowd.] "We advocate that all black people get some guns and learn to use them. The only way to get Kennedy Hill off the force is to organize the black power in this area and use your guns. [Officers drive by.] Black Power! [The officers are three in one car. The driver passes, turns around, drives by again.] Black Power! [The driver of the car reversed the car.] Black Power!

Kennedy Hill: [Pointing his finger at Carmichael as he hopped out of the car.] "Listen you. You don't go 'round shouting and going on, hear?"

Carmichael: "Would you like to speak to me? I'm Mr. Carmichael."

Hill: "I don't give a damn who you are! You've got no business shouting like that."

Carmichael: [To crowd.] "You know, the only time black people are allowed to meet without interference is to pray and to dance. Whenever black people get together for any other reasons, the honkies get scared and come out to beat and kill us."

Hill: "Shut up, boy, 'cause I'm the law around here."

Carmichael: "Take off that tin badge and drop your gun. I'll show you something, honkie."

Hill: "You're threatening me."

Carmichael: "Do you want to arrest me?"

Hill: "No, we don't want to arrest you. Our job is to protect the people."

Carmichael: "Just drop your tin badge and that gun, honkie. [Then to crowd.] These honkies want to send us to Vietnam to fight the Viet Cong and then they get all the credit. Our war is right here in the United States of America, black people."

[More policemen came.]

Carmichael: "From now on, it's going to be an eye for an eye, a tooth for a tooth, and a honkie for every black man killed!"

Hill: "You're under arrest!"[25]

HILL STRUCK CARMICHAEL AFTER securing him in a police car, jerked a camera from the neck of a photographer for a civil rights newspaper, *The Southern Courier*, and snatched a tape recorder from Norman Lumpkin, a radio news reporter. The protestors then moved their meeting from the church yard to the yard of Dan Houser's nearby house.[26]

Within five minutes—around "first dark"—gunshots fired from the vicinity of a police car patrolling the area scattered the crowd and about forty people, including Houser, took cover inside the house. In the words of Judge Frank M. Johnson, Jr., following a four-day hearing the same year in October, "[u]ntil about 2:00 A.M. on Monday, June 12, Prattville, Alabama, literally became an armed camp."[27]

State troopers, Autauga County deputies, Prattville policemen, and Alabama National Guardsmen surrounded Houser's house, where

Sheriff Phillip Wood used a loudspeaker to order everyone outside. Officers allowed most to go home or stay inside Houser's house, but they arrested Houser and almost a dozen others. All but Houser were taken to the Autauga County Jail.

Prattville police officers placed Houser in a police car and took him straight to the Prattville city jail. Prior to his release late the next day, without being charged with any crime, Houser "was severely beaten about the face, head and body either by Prattville police officers or, with [their] knowledge and consent, by someone else."[28]

Houser's injuries kept him hospitalized for several days in Montgomery's St. Jude's Hospital. When I saw him, I had no doubt that the specter of "Bert & Dan" incited the suspected Ku Klux Klan assailants.[29]

17

THE OTHER SIDE OF THE BATTLE

Y'all can't arrest me—I'm a white man!"

Hobson City was the wrong place in the 1970s for an intoxicated, speeding motorist daring to pull rank on black police officers by touting his mixed blood, especially since the State of Alabama colored him the same as them.[30] Ronald L. Veldhousen, on the night of September 2, 1979, learned that lesson—painfully, brutally, and doubtless in response to the racial exemption he wrongly claimed.

Nestled in Calhoun County's southeastern valley between Anniston and Oxford, Hobson City incorporated in 1889 as the first "Negro" town in Alabama. Originally called "Lick Skillet," the town measures just over a square mile and has never counted more than nine hundred citizens. In stark contrast to its bordering neighbors, however, blacks have always made up at least 90 percent of Hobson City's population.[31]

Veldhousen had sped through the overhead "caution" light downtown on Broad Street—since renamed Martin Luther King Drive. Told that he was drunk and speeding recklessly, an incensed Veldhousen displayed a righteous indignation which landed him in the cruiser under arrest for assaulting a police officer, reckless driving, and DUI.

Because Hobson City had no jail of its own, the officers transported

Veldhousen to the Oxford police station, where the jailers took one look at his white skin, the policemen's black skin, and declined to hold him. Finally secured in Anniston at the Calhoun County jail, Veldhousen suffered a severe beating at the hands of Hobson City police officers. In the federal lawsuit filed six months later, he described an unprovoked attack:

> . . . on or about September 2, 1979, while in the custody of the defendants and while handcuffed, defendants did commit an assault and battery on him by hitting, striking, or beating him with their fists and a billy club or a blackjack on or about his head, eyes, nose, forehead, back, chest, ribs, thighs, calves, and legs, thereby causing lacerations and hemorrhaging around and to Plaintiff's right eye, severe bruises to his nose, lacerations and contusions on his left forehead, contusions over and upon his left and right rib cage, contusions around the right castovertebral angle area and over and upon the vertebrae, contusions over and upon both his thighs, and contusions over and upon the calves of both his legs.[32]

For these injuries which hospitalized him for a week, Veldhousen sought $500,000 from the three officers allegedly responsible.[33]

HOBSON CITY—A LONGTIME CLIENT on the school desegregation battleground[34]—retained me to defend the lawsuit. The sued officers made up almost the entire police force, and the city also boasted a black female mayor and an all-black city council. What the city did not have was a black lawyer. A days-long trial ended with a jury verdict in favor of two officers and against the third for only one dollar as damages.

It was a hollow victory in which I took no pride.

The pictures of Veldhousen's battered body and his medical reports told the real story, and they left me with the uneasy feeling that the policemen really enjoyed themselves as they beat the hapless man.

After replaying the trial in my mind, as I always do, I concluded that I could not attribute the "victory" to my trial skills or strategy. The sad reality is that Veldhousen's lawyer made some colossal mistakes, starting with his failure to name either Hobson City or Calhoun County as defendants.

Not long after the verdict, I demanded that the mayor assemble the city council to meet with me. In no uncertain terms, I read them the riot act on "equal protection of the laws." Not a one left without understanding the plain illegality and moral wrongness of the vicious beating inflicted gratuitously by their police officers.

On the drive home to Montgomery, I reflected on the many "police brutality" cases I had pursued to vindicate atrocious misconduct by white officers against blacks. Save for a single homicide, none rivaled the injuries inflicted on Veldhousen. Then and there, I vowed never again, under any circumstances, to be on "the other side of the battle."

18

Freedom Riders and a Slow Delivery

The dawn's early light on May 20, 1961, found me in my favorite fishing spot on the banks of the creek flowing below my back yard. A perfect Saturday morning respite from the civil rights battlefield.

Before my doodle pole could snare a single keeper catfish, Uncle John[35] shattered my tranquil space with an urgent report. A belligerent gang of whites attacked a busload of "Freedom Riders" as soon as they arrived at the Greyhound bus terminal adjacent to the federal courthouse in downtown Montgomery; the continuing assaults were brutal, indiscriminate, and unrestrained by law enforcement.

I dressed hurriedly and made a quick stop at my office before rushing to the bus station.

The "serious riot"[36] had subsided when I arrived. I immediately spotted my sister, Dr. Hagalyn Seay Wilson,[37] calmly attending to the injured, clearly oblivious to her own danger. Her nurse in the office which then adjoined mine told me that she had sprinted out with her medical bag as soon as she heard about the riot.

"Are you crazy?" I hollered at her. Barely glancing up from the bloodied man on the ground, she mumbled, "One does what one has to do." The only doctor at the scene, she helped as many as she could before escorting the severely beaten to St. Jude's Hospital.[38]

Many of those assaulted had not been on the bus. A young black man walking to work eagerly jumped in when he saw several thugs passionately pounding a black girl. Battered and bruised just as badly for his valor, he seemed surprisingly upbeat when I stopped by his hospital bed. "I'll be all right," he told me, "but there are some white boys out there somewhere who are in a hell of a lot worse shape than me."

I regret that I did not preserve this young man's name; he certainly deserves enshrinement as a hero more than so many self-proclaimed "giants of the movement."

SATURDAY'S TURMOIL AT THE bus station triggered a logistically challenging week and the busiest period of my entire legal career. On the home front, a richly pregnant Ettra with an "any day now" due date kept me on guard. My mother rushed her to the hospital on Sunday morning. False alarm!

Law partner Fred Gray and I made the office our home. More freedom riders—black and white, male and female—flocked into the city every day. They were routinely arrested as soon as they got off the bus. We perfected our routine: interview each person arrested, secure bonds for anyone who preferred to be released immediately, make arrangements for the reasonable comfort of those choosing to remain jailed for awhile.

First Baptist Church, led by the Reverend Ralph D. Abernathy, hosted a huge mass meeting on Sunday evening. Many of the injured and released freedom riders appeared. An angry white mob, much larger than the gang which accosted the first bus, filled the Ripley

Street area in front of the church; however, they scrupulously avoided the northern boundary which faced the all-black Trenholm Court housing project.

The vigilantes, including a fair number of robed Klansmen, wreaked havoc all night long. They overturned and set on fire several cars parked outside the church; one belonged to Virginia Durr, a white activist who, along with her lawyer-husband Clifford, proudly supported the movement.

Inside, the masses settled comfortably and confidently in the main sanctuary and in the basement, uplifted through the night by songs, prayers, and preaching.[39] In the wee hours of Monday morning, they safely exited a church now encircled by National Guardsmen called into service with the declaration of limited martial law.

THE CITY REMAINED UNDER martial law for several days while buses rolled in and out with freedom riders. Fred and I toiled away at our law office and in the county jail.

On Monday, the third day of freedom rides, Sheriff Mac Sim Butler called with news I could use.

"You may want to come pick up your buddies we just arrested," he said. "They say they're lawyers from New York—Percy Sutton, he's black, and the other one is a white man, Mark Lane."

I couldn't wait to get them out and in the office to help manage the mounting assortment of legal tasks. Sutton quickly dampened my enthusiasm.

"Son," he looked up at me, "how old are you?"

"Twenty-nine," I replied.

"How long have you been practicing law?"

"About three and a half years."

Sutton shook his head and smiled. "It is simply amazing how fast you young black lawyers in the South develop. I have been practicing law for eleven years and I have not tried three cases in the federal courts. We can't be of any help to you, son. Anyway, we're headed for Jackson, Mississippi."[40]

I didn't have time to wallow in my genuine disappointment.

Early the next morning, Mother again rushed Ettra to the hospital. Another false alarm, but this time she decided to stay.

MEANWHILE, REVEREND ABERNATHY GOT arrested with freedom riders who sat at the white lunch counter inside the Trailways bus terminal. His wife, Juanita, called me the next morning to secure something for him. When I arrived from the office which had been my home since Saturday night, she handed me a fully packed suitcase.

"I don't know if the sheriff will allow this," I tried to explain jailhouse protocol, "but I will give it a try."

The sheriff responded directly and decently: "I'll give it to him." He returned momentarily and related Reverend Abernathy's request to talk with me.

Within half an hour Reverend Abernathy strutted out, rubbing lotion on his hands, decked out in a three-piece suit, starched shirt with cuff links, and a silk tie. Sheriff Butler looked first at me and then at Ralph before letting loose a hearty laugh.

"What the hell is so funny?" I asked.

"Seay, if I didn't know any better, I would swear that we had you in custody, and Reverend Abernathy is the slick Philadelphia lawyer who came down South to spring you."

I knew then it was past time for a ride out to my house for a quick shower. As I approached my driveway late that night, a military jeep blocked my path and three uniformed "soldiers" assumed a ready stance next to a 105mm recoilless rifle pointed at my house. I turned around and started up the road to my dad's house, only to discover another staffed jeep parked in his driveway.

Back in Montgomery, I immediately went to Sheriff Butler. When he explained that the units were ordered for our protection, I responded, "but those are the guys that I don't trust."

Sheriff Mac promptly had the National Guard troops removed and replaced them with deputy sheriffs in clearly marked sheriff's vehicles.

On her second day in the hospital—and the fifth day of freedom rides—Ettra called me crying. Placed initially in the maternity ward, she had been transferred to a private room by the well-meaning nun-director who recognized her. There she was lonely and more fearful. After arranging for her return to the ward, I scurried back to the office.

MEANWHILE, SOME OF THE freedom riders who had arrived the first day had succeeded in integrating one of the terminal's lunch counters. We filed our federal complaint the next day, May 25, and much later that day, the sheriff—pursuant to instructions from the National Guard commander—arrested another interracial group as they waited in vain to be served at the same counter.[41]

Among the ten arrested were ministers Wyatt T. Walker and Fred L. Shuttlesworth; student activist Bernard Lee; William Sloane Coffin, the Yale chaplain who championed civil rights and peace movements; and a handful of religion professors from New England colleges. Because they landed in jail well after the last meal call, they were pretty irritable when Fred and I arrived.

When someone asked if they could send out for food, Sheriff Mac shocked them, I suspect, with his response: "Why don't y'all make a list of whatever you want and give it to Fred. I'll take him to pick it up, and Seay can stay here and take care of business."

Coffin hungered at that moment to retrieve from a not-so-friendly deputy the reading material confiscated at his arrest. He struck a menacing pose in military-style jacket, pants, and boots, and appeared to be in great shape. When he threatened to "thrash" the offending deputy if he did not return his papers—"and I mean right now"—the sheriff calmly ordered the deputy to comply.

Fred and the sheriff returned with grocery bags filled with bologna, ice cream bars, cookies, peanut butter crackers, potato chips, and other junk food. "Seay," Sheriff Mac called out to me, "I should have taken you instead of Fred. When we got ready to check out with all this stuff, Fred claimed he didn't have but two dollars. I had to pay for the rest!"

After the freedom riders consumed all they wanted, Sheriff Mac told his deputies to distribute the rest of the goodies to others in custody.

I TOOK MY WEARY body to the hospital. Notwithstanding the late hour, Ettra was wide awake, calm, and overly concerned about my welfare. Just sleeping in the chair by her bedside relieved my fatigue.

I awoke to find Ettra still richly pregnant, and after an hour or so, I concluded that my presence would not hasten her delivery. Back to the office and a new round of freedom riders. When I finally finished my routine, I headed straight to Madison Park and the comfort of my own bed.

JOY on the Eighth Day!

The phone rang early on May 27, 1961, around the same time that, eight days earlier, the news of brutal assaults on the first bus of freedom riders had interrupted my peaceful quest for catfish from the creek.

"It's a girl," greeted me softly before I could say hello.

I made it to the hospital in record time and gazed upon the most beautiful sight I had seen all week, all month, all year: Yalise Yvette Seay. Mother and baby girl were both just fine, my sister assured me, and within hours, I proudly drove them home.

19

Marengo County

For almost two decades, starting around 1966, the legal battle to desegregate Alabama's public elementary and secondary schools practically consumed my practice. I partnered with Fred Gray soon after he successfully sued to integrate public schools in Macon County. *Lee v. Macon County Board of Education*[42] required Alabama officials to implement the Supreme Court's mandate in *Brown v. Board of Education*.[43]

Only in Alabama did lawyers seek to use a single case to desegregate every public school system in the state. Governors and state superintendents—so vitriolic in their "segregation today, segregation tomorrow, and segregation forever" defiance—facilitated the effort. Eventually, our firm handled federal lawsuits involving ninety-nine school systems governed by *Lee v. Macon*, and I became quite familiar with the highways and byways in all but a handful of the state's sixty-seven counties.[44]

In addition to state-sponsored opposition to court-ordered integration, entrenched resistance in cities and counties permeated every layer of the all-white power structures. The most mean-spirited adversaries in the mid-1960s and 1970s controlled the counties in central Alabama's Black Belt.

Two defining features marked these mainly rural counties—fertile, coal-black, cotton-growing soil; and a majority population of poor and powerless blacks.

Mᴀʀᴇɴɢᴏ Cᴏᴜɴᴛʏ ꜰᴏᴜɢʜᴛ ʜᴀʀᴅᴇʀ than any other school system to maintain segregated schools. The county operated three separately funded and staffed systems—Linden City Schools, Demopolis City Schools, and Marengo County Schools; each maintained different schools for blacks and whites. *Lee v. Macon* required desegregation plans to end these dual systems.

Fred D. Ramsay, superintendent of the Marengo County school system, single-handedly made our desegregation effort there the most contentious, challenging, and unpleasant experience I encountered in the entire state. Our first conversation in late 1967 preceded a planning conference in federal court, and it pretty much set the tone for a decade-long, bitter struggle.

A huge man—around six feet seven inches tall and two hundred and fifty pounds—Ramsey approached me with an extended hand, cordially introduced himself, and launched into a defense of segregated schools. "Now, I'm not a racist, Seay," he ended gratuitously.

"Well, Mr. Ramsey," I looked straight in his eyes, "I do know you don't believe in integration. The good white folks in Marengo County would not let you remain in office if you did. So, if you don't believe in integration, and you personally are not a racist, there is but one place left for you to hang your hat, and that's slavery."

Reputedly a professional fighter in his youth, Ramsay allowed his huge hands to feel the muscles in both my arms before he joked, "Seay, slavery is history, but if we still had slavery, I sure would like to own you."

I retorted just as quickly and did not crack a smile: "I don't think so, Mr. Ramsey. You see, while I might look rather strong, I really can't stand a lot of sunshine and heat. So you would have to make a house nigger out of me, and I don't think you would want this big black buck anywhere around the big house."

Grudging respect marked our subsequent communications. Ramsay reserved his most abusive tirades for my lawyer colleagues from the U.S. Department of Justice, while they were constrained not to respond on strict orders from the Attorney General.

THE CYCLE OF REJECTED, modified, or ignored desegregation plans continued until mid-1970, when Marengo County's *Lee v. Macon* counterpart came under the supervision of U.S. District Judge Daniel H. Thomas, sitting in the Southern District of Alabama. Acting ex parte, Judge Thomas approved a patently inadequate plan proposed by the school board. An appellate court vacated the order and directed him to require a comprehensive plan with specified levels of student, faculty, and staff desegregation, along with policies for student transfers, transportation, school construction, and monitoring reports.

Again, the school board submitted an unacceptable plan, but three days later and without a hearing, Judge Thomas ordered it implemented. The predictable reversal on appeal ordered him either to adopt the government's proposed plan or require the school board to demonstrate its unworkability and to submit an alternative, effective plan. A wily Superintendent Ramsey seized upon these instructions to orchestrate, in early 1973, a massive letter-writing campaign by teachers, staff, parents, and concerned citizens—black and white—denouncing any plan forcing school integration.

Hundreds of letters poured into my office, all directed to me as "NEA" attorney.[45] They were, in the main, well-written and laudatory affirmations of the status quo interspersed with dire predictions of doom for the school system under our desegregation plan. I held on to some of the more poignant, paternalistic, and plainly ridiculous letters.

Not surprisingly, many white parents expressed passed-down fears for their children being in the minority and in the presence of black boys. One wrote:

> I have four white children going to school at Marengo County High in Thomaston. We live out in the County eight miles from town. The original plan had my 4 kids going to four different schools. Each one of them they would be outnumbered 3 to 1. At the high school my little girl would have attended the ratio there would be 5 to 1. She is not quite 5 ft. tall, doesn't weigh a 100 lbs. Some of the boys or men, Negro boys that is, are 20 years old or older. Some of them have at least two children or more. I am afraid I would be scared to death all the time. Is that what public education is all about? Parents being scared all day while their children are attending school. If you and Judge Hand can see fit to give us a ruling that we can live with please do so. If not I and others like me will try to send our kids to private schools.

Another common theme—resentment at the federal government's interference with an allegedly acceptable way of life—resounded just as frequently, as illustrated by these excerpts from various letters:

> I was raised up on a farm with colored people and played in the sand with them all of my childhood. Some colored people today would fight you or anyone else about me. About eighty per cent of the colored people in Marengo County are happy with the school

system we have at present. They really have better schools than some of the whites. I believe in letting pupils, black or white, go to the school of their choice, which ever they perfer. The colored people as well as white don't believe in sending their children across town when there is a school in their front yard. If things keep on going as they are now sooner or later there won't be any education. We parents have no more say so over our children.

I believe in equality for all but a child without an education cannot have equal rights and opportunities, and children, whether white or colored, cannot get the proper education in unpleasant situations and it is unpleasant when they are sent or forced to go to schools where they are unhappy. If you integrate Marengo County in a percentage or ratio manner without giving any choice, they will be unhappy and there will be no education for negroes or whites.

I suspect that economic pressures dictated the letter from a black man who struggled with his grammar and spelling as he enumerated twelve separate "points why we want to keep our school all Black." I received at least three handwritten and signed letters with precisely the same language:

1. We would like for the Black to be to gather.
2. We would like for the White to be to gather
3. The Black or White would get along to gather.
4. They would get there lesson.
5. I don't feel like the White or the Black have anything in common.
6. We Black love our school and would like to keep it Black.

7. The Black don't want the H.E.W. plan in Marengo at all.

8. We Black need our jobs.

9. The White will be mean to the Black. And the Black will be mean to the White.

10. So many Black cant get job.

11. So many Black in Marengo the White wont give jobs.

12. The White don't want the Black. And Black don't want the White.

Superintendent Ramsay contributed to the plethora of negative letters, sending them not only to me but also to the federal judge, the attorney general, Justice Department lawyers, and Alabama's congressional delegation. In a September 4, 1974, letter (also copied to President Gerald Ford), he chastised "uninformed or ignorant bureaucrats" at the Justice Department for

> caus[ing] this system to spend thousands of dollars that were sorely needed for educational purposes and are causing this school system to continue excessive busing several times daily to simply satisfy your desire for racial balances although this school system is far more integrated than any other system in this area and probably more so than any system in the Country, particularly those northern and eastern school systems that the Justice Department seems to ignore.[46]

RAMSAY DID NOT STOP with his letter-writing campaign but seized every opportunity to create chaos and to portray the plaintiffs' lawyers as the villains. He orchestrated one especially galling incident just before his scheduled deposition at a courthouse in Linden. Ramsay sent word that he needed first to confer with the attorneys; everyone else ignored the request. Motivated solely by curiosity, I proceeded to a conference room packed, to my surprise, with two dozen or more black teachers and principals. After introducing me as the NEA's lawyer, he angrily shouted at me:

"Lawyer Seay, these people are all my good friends. I asked them to come down here so you can explain to them what the NEA plans to do to help them feed their families when you and the Justice Department succeed in shutting down the school system and leaving them with no jobs."

Only the grace of God kept me from exploding. I walked out without a word.

Hugh Lloyd, lawyer for all the school systems in Marengo County, proved a welcome contrast to Superintendent Ramsay. Extremely competent and a story-book Southern gentleman, he often engaged me in really interesting conversations. When he invited me to dinner after the early end of depositions one day, I did not hesitate.

White tablecloths and cloth napkins adorned dining tables at the Demopolis Hotel on the town square, and the silverware had the feel of real silver. Who would have guessed?

Lloyd knew everybody, and the diners who came by to greet him acknowledged me pleasantly. Following a sumptuous meal, I met the chubby cook, a young black woman clearly delighted to see me. That meal may have been my best experience in Marengo County.

THE NEXT DAY I went back for lunch and stopped afterwards at the barbershop I'd glimpsed after dinner. Two smocked barbers graced the sparkling clean shop tucked in a corner of the hotel lobby—a black man, cutting a white patron's hair, and a black woman standing idly by her chair in an otherwise empty shop. I took off my coat and sauntered toward the woman. "Can I get a haircut?"

"Sir, I can't cut your hair." Nothing in her face or voice communicated the problem.

"Why?"

"I have not been trained to cut your hair," she replied.

"That's okay," I assured her, "here is your chance to get some on-the-job training cutting a man's hair, and I don't mind."

The slightly irritable voice of her co-barber husband broke an awkward silence: "Why don't you just tell the man the truth? We don't cut colored folks' hair."

Stunned and momentarily speechless, I looked straight at him: "Give me that again?"

"I said, we don't cut colored folks hair."

I gave him a long stare. "Well, is there a barber shop in the city of Demopolis where a colored man can get a haircut?" He gave me directions to a black barber shop on the far side of town.

As I sat later in the cross-town barber shop, I pondered my next move. I had tried and won "public accommodations" discrimination lawsuits across the state. I had also never been shy to act whenever I felt victimized. When the governor declined to renew my license as a notary public, I sued for discrimination and refused to back down even after Judge Johnson chastised me, in chambers, for "wasting time with such a trivial lawsuit." When the restaurant inside the Heart of Camden Motel in Wilcox County refused to serve me for lunch, I prevailed in my lawsuit.

Why was I reluctant now to act? The black barbers' refusal to cut my hair solely on account on my race was a clear-cut case of discrimination in a place of public accommodations.

I am not proud that I did nothing. Regardless of the perpetrator's race, discrimination on account of race, color, or ethnicity is morally and legally wrong, and it should not be tolerated without a fight.

WITH THE *Lee v. Macon* litigation still pending against the Board of Education, another group of blacks in Marengo County initiated a federal redistricting lawsuit aimed at integrating the all-white board. The United States joined in as plaintiff-intervenor and called me as a witness at the federal court hearing in Selma.

After documenting my lawyer's role in the cases to desegregate most of the state's school systems, I declared unequivocally Marengo County's all-white school board and its superintendent as the most insensitive and recalcitrant I ever confronted. The judge turned to me after the lawyers completed their examination.

"Seay," he spoke sincerely, "do you think we will ever solve the problems of race in this country?"

"Sure," I responded, "because ever is a long, long time, and it is bound to happen—ever; but it will not happen in your lifetime or mine."

With a quizzical look, he persisted. "Why?"

I pondered my answer very carefully. "Judge, I'm really not sure, but perhaps it's just that I've been black too long and you've been white too long."

A hush fell over the courtroom. Momentarily, the bailiff announced a recess for fifteen minutes.

While I stood in the hall talking to a Justice Department lawyer, Superintendent Ramsay stormed directly in front of me, shook his finger in my face, and screamed, "God damn you, Seay, you told a damned lie on me."

I could not believe his gall. In the hallway crowded mainly with blacks, I knew I could not let this go unchallenged. Pushing aside another lawyer who quickly stepped between us, I took a step or two backwards, put my finger in Ramsay's face, and spoke loudly with a controlled tone.

"If you don't know what the f— you're doing, you better ask somebody, because this crazy-ass nigger will kick your ass."

Within seconds the bailiff firmly grasped my arm and escorted me into the judge's chambers. Curiously, the judge had heard only my response to Ramsay. I apologized but also announced, respectfully, that I simply would not allow anyone to accost me anywhere, as Ramsay did, without retaliating in kind. To preclude any further confrontations, the court granted my request to remain seated in the courtroom for the remainder of the trial.

Ramsay resigned as superintendent not long after that trial. In typical fashion, he went out with a flare. In a lengthy newspaper article, prominently featuring his full-body photograph, he recounted his various efforts to preserve the school system and predicted its demise under the desegregation plans pushed by those "Dick Tracy lawyers from the Injustice Department in Washington, D.C." and that "Mickey Mouse lawyer from Montgomery, Alabama."

I actually took a liking to that "Mickey Mouse" moniker and became a collector of memorabilia from all over the world. One of my most prized items is a very, very old Mickey Mouse box camera; I got it from a photojournalist whose works were featured in several national newspapers and magazines. His grandmother had given it to him as a birthday present. It still takes pictures . . . if you can find the film.

PART FIVE

ALL IN THE FAMILY

"It is not what you are called,
but what you answer to."

— *African proverb*

Solomon and Ettra Seay, on their wedding day.

20

WHAT'S IN A NAME?

S o it is with great pleasure that I present to you our Law Day speaker this year, one of the most respected civil rights lawyers in this state: Solomon S. Seay *(See)*, Jr."

At the end of my speech at the Montgomery County Bar Association's annual meeting on May 1, 2001, the presiding judge of the Montgomery County Circuit Court—a long-time friend and the first African American to grace the county's judiciary—stood for closing remarks.

"Now, if I had introduced our guest speaker as Attorney *Say,* he would have corrected me immediately. Black folks have to call him Attorney *See,* you know, but he will let white folks address him as *Say.* What's up with that, Sol?"

Judge Charles Price could be counted on to add a little levity to any occasion. I declined, with a smile, his invitation to banter.

The correct pronunciation of my surname is a question I confronted long before I became a lawyer. I made it through my seventh birthday pronouncing it exactly like I heard it from the family, neighbors, and church folk in Alabama. They called my father, Reverend Solomon S. Seay, Sr., "Preacher *See,*" and we children were Preacher *See's* kids.

Daddy preached at central and south Alabama churches within the African Methodist Episcopal Zion denomination, and he also headed the connection's Lomax Hannon School in Butler County. Our family moved to Greensboro, North Carolina, shortly after I turned eight, and there we heard a strange pronunciation, "*See-a*." It required a major adjustment which took most of our four years in Greensboro, but all of us, Daddy included, finally made the transition from *See* to *See-a*.

Black Methodist preachers seldom enjoy long tenures at a single church, and Daddy's assignments fit the norm. Four years after embracing ourselves as Preacher *See-a*'s kids, we were off to the largest A.M.E. Zion church in Knoxville, Tennessee. *Seay*, in Tennessee, was *Say*, and perhaps because it had a stronger, more regal sound, and was much easier to pronounce, the whole family quickly dropped *See-a* for *Say*.

In 1948, the denomination transferred my father from Knoxville to Mount Zion A.M.E. Zion Church in Montgomery, and he brought back to Alabama the "*Say*" pronunciation which fastened to him for the remainder of his preaching and civil rights journey.

In the summer of 1948, I worked on a tobacco farm in Connecticut, along with a number of black students from many Southern colleges; no one took exception to the *Say* pronunciation, and it accompanied me through college, the military, several summer jobs in Ohio, and law school. I returned to Montgomery in June 1957 as Solomon S. Seay ("*Say*"), Jr.

Everyone in the black community pronounced our name "*Say*," and we appeared to be the only Seay family in town. I remained comfortable with that pronunciation until I started to practice law and discovered another Seay—Noble Seay, clerk of the Supreme Court of Alabama. He and seemingly all within the white community pronounced his name "*See*."

WHAT'S IN A NAME?

The largely white courthouse crowd—no doubt accustomed to Clerk Seay—insisted on referring to me as "*See*" while the more familiar "*Say*" pronunciation resonated in the black community. "Lawyer *See*'s office" confused a black caller as much as "Lawyer *Say*'s office" confounded white callers. As a matter of convenience, I accommodated both preferences as the community or the occasion dictated, but vacillating between *See* and *Say* became more than a little cumbersome for me.

My daughter Yalise called me from school one day and asked me to drop off the lunch money she had forgotten. I left a dollar with the assistant principal for Yalise "*See*." As soon as I walked through the door at home later that evening, Yalise started fussing about having had to borrow her lunch money from a teacher. I assured her that I had delivered a dollar for her lunch. "Daddy," she pondered after awhile, "I did hear an announcement over the intercom for Yalise *See*, but I didn't know they were talking about me."

I decided then to make a choice. Much to the chagrin of my father who incorrectly viewed it as a sign of disrespect, I opted for "*See*." For me, it just seemed to flow more easily than "*Say*."

Ettra gravitated much more slowly to "*See*," but my kids never made the change from "*Say*." It matters not to me. Our name is Seay; only our deeds will honor my father's legacy.

21

PLOWING WITH PRIDE

I looked a mess and felt just as bad.

Hauled into federal court by an armed deputy marshal who refused to give me any time to get presentable . . . on orders from Judge Frank M. Johnson, Jr., that he find and bring me to court "right now, just as you are!" And so I stood before the bench in his huge and majestic courtroom—in combat boots, dusty fatigues, and a skivvy shirt thoroughly soiled, as were my face and hands, from hours of plowing in my dad's cotton fields.

"Mr. Seay," Judge Johnson glowered down at me through those little eyeglasses half on his nose, "why were you not here with your client when I sounded the docket this morning?"

The lyrics from an old blues tune had come to mind as soon as I saw the judge take his seat: *"Good Morning, Judge! Why do you look so mean? If there's any trouble, I'll plead not guilty, it must be someone else because you know it can't be me."*

"Good morning, Judge," I started. Silence and a steely gaze confirmed that I should have skipped the greeting.

"Your Honor," I continued, "I was not supposed to have a case on your docket this morning."

When he named the indigent defendant, a young man charged with interstate transportation of a stolen motor vehicle, I related the prosecuting attorney's agreement to continue the case from the scheduled docket so that I could file a motion to have my client undergo a psychological evaluation. Fortunately, the assistant U.S. attorney, also summoned, confirmed our communications and took the heat for failing to notify his substitute at the docket call. Neither of us knew that my incarcerated client had insisted that the deputies bring him in from the city jail to enter a guilty plea against my advice.

"All right, Seay," Judge Johnson softened just a bit, "you can go back to plowing. The marshal will take you home, but you get that motion filed tomorrow."

"You have a good morning, Judge," I returned his slight smile.

THE TIME I SPENT plowing cotton, in 1962, had everything to do with my father's tenacious pride, a defining trait I inherited. His determination to have his own and to support his own probably got ingrained by his parents on the rural Macon County plantation they sharecropped to raise twenty-one children.

"Before I will compromise what I believe in," Dad often said, "even at the expense of a life in abject poverty, I will stand on my head in a corner and stack BBs for a living, and that's as hard a job as any man can have."

Farming supplemented my dad's meager earnings from the ministry. My mother inherited a lot of land which qualified for a cotton allotment under the Agricultural Adjustment Act of 1938, administered locally by County Agricultural Committees. Dad planted around twenty acres of cotton each year and secured advance payments from the government in the form of non-recourse loans; the government paid more than the market price at the time of sale.

In the early spring of 1962, Dad reported to the government

warehouse for the usual financing of the next crop. This time the warehouse manager greeted him strangely, with an apology: "Rev, I'm sorry, but I can't handle it this year."

"Why?" Dad asked.

"I just can't handle it this year."

My father reminded him of their cordial relationship doing business for several years. "I don't understand. I have never had a bad year, and the good Lord willing, this year will be same."

The warehouseman could only nod his head. "I know, Reverend. I'm sorry, but I just can't handle it this year."

Dad did not ask another question. "I understand," he said, and left.

A few months earlier, in December 1961, Dad had become president of the Montgomery Improvement Association. His inaugural address included a strong call for integration of the city's public schools and reopening of public parks closed by city officials in defiance of court-ordered integration.

It could have been Dad's leadership in the organization which launched the bus boycott and continued the push for desegregation, or it might have been my highly visible role as a movement attorney; either or both, we understood.

That very evening the family gathered at my father's house to discuss the financial consequences of the wrongfully denied subsidy for Dad's cotton farming.

The federal Act allowed Dad to lease his allotment for redistribution by the County Agricultural Committee, but he never entertained the option.

We all decided that he would not stand on his head in that corner and stack BBs alone. To supplement her monthly teaching salary,

Mom contracted with Whitfield Pickle Company to raise six acres of cucumbers; she hired all the neighborhood kids as pickle pickers.

Though I had spent the bulk of my time behind a desk or in court, I still knew how to operate a Farmall Cub tractor with a double buster harrow. But I never learned to plow a straight row with a mule.

22

Never a Mumbling Word

My dad lived in a modest brick house within shouting distance of mine. One afternoon following lunch he stepped outside his front door, picking his teeth with a stick match. A gunshot sounded, and a small-caliber bullet ripped through Dad's right arm, ricocheted off a bone, and raced about eight inches up his fleshy forearm.

Fortunately, his habitual after-meal toothpick in his upraised hand put his arm in position to thwart the bullet's targeted path to his heart.

Fred Gray and I had just finished a hearing in federal court. As we stood outside waiting for the traffic signal to change, a young white lawyer braked his car at the corner and yelled out the window to me, "Sol, I am glad to see you were not seriously injured."

My puzzled look elicited the news report just broadcast on the radio: "Lawyer Solomon Seay has just been shot; no word yet on his condition."

Fred looked at me, I looked at him, and without uttering a word, we struck a trot for our office to drive out to Dad's. We processed the report from home as we rushed into my car: Dad had indeed been shot, the injury was not life-threatening, and he had been taken straight to Dr. Jefferson Underwood's office.

The shooters—three teen-aged white boys—prepared for their ambush from a car parked about 150 feet from Dad's house. Though identified and arrested, not one has ever been prosecuted, a fact never explained to Dad or anyone else in the family.

With his doctor's concurrence, Dad decided to let the bullet alone unless and until it caused serious problems. He lived for the rest of his life with that bullet lodged in his arm.

I LEARNED ONLY IN recent years—long after the shooting—that Dad took a bullet intended for me.

Police investigators shared this fact with Dad promptly after interviewing the teenagers. Dad later related it to my wife Ettra and to my lawyer-nephew, James Wilson, who frequently chauffeured him around for speaking engagements.

When James finally told me, I asked Ettra why she had kept me in the dark. She answered simply and without apology: "You did not need to know—and more importantly—you did not need to know that I knew."

That was just her way.

Ettra was an absolutely fearless woman. To my surprise, she confessed—long, long after we weathered the stormy years of my practice—just how much she feared for me on my frequent late-night forays across rural Alabama to defend teacher termination cases.

But she never said a mumbling word.

23

FLUTE LIPS

She was nine months old when I first laid eyes on her. Just one look, and I tagged her with the nickname which bonded us specially for the next fourteen years, "Skinny."

I was somewhere in the Austrian Alps stationed with an infantry unit when Ettra delivered our first child on September 29, 1954, in a hospital room at Montgomery's Maxwell Air Force Base. She named her Sheryl Denise.

Even as a toddler Skinny loved to tag along behind me, she tried to mimic me, and she wanted to have everything she saw in my hands. Some called her a daddy's girl.

I came home one afternoon chomping on a pickled pig's foot. I absolutely treasured this underappreciated delicacy. Skinny began begging as soon as she saw me.

"Just let me have a little bite, Daddy."

"You don't want any of this, Skinny, trust me." Oblivious to my warning, she kept whining until I finally relented.

"Here," I thrust the pig's foot into her mouth, "go on and take your bite."

Just as I expected, Skinny could not bear to stomach even a little bite and handed it back to me in a hot second. Not to lose a "teaching moment," I made her finish the morsel she bit and the remainder I savored. Tears streaming, she managed to pull it off without regurgitating. Today she refuses to be even in the proximity of a pig's foot.

WE SENT SKINNY TO private schools for kindergarten through third grade. Wanting her also to experience the unique benefits of public school, we switched her to Carver Elementary School for fourth through sixth grades. Then almost a decade after the U.S. Supreme Court outlawed racial segregation in public schools, Alabama's schools at every level remained rigidly separate with the equities in facilities and resources disproportionately favoring white schools.

Still searching for the best academic fit, we chose the private Laboratory School at Alabama State College (now Alabama State University) for Skinny's transition to junior high school. She started seventh grade in the fall of 1965 just as Montgomery County prepared to operate its first term of court-ordered desegregation in all grades. Under the system's plan of gradual integration, only three black students enrolled in 1964 at each of the city's white high schools, Robert E. Lee and Sidney Lanier. The numbers—all blacks choosing to attend white schools, never vice versa—increased gradually each term.

Our Madison Park home fell within the neighborhoods zoned for Goodwyn Junior High School. In her eighth grade year, Skinny enrolled as its first black student. First, I indoctrinated her thoroughly in my principles of permissible conduct:

You have a God-given right to defend yourself. In fact, the Good Lord gave every animal, including man, a means to defend himself. Mistreat a dog and he will bite; stir up a bee's nest, and the bees will sting; scare a skunk, and he will fire up your nostrils from a great distance. Now if somebody wants to engage you in a rational discussion, then you can sit down and converse rationally. But if someone calls you a dirty name, I

*want you to retort with something that is equally dirty. If he puts his hand
on you inappropriately, I expect you to get anything you can in your hand
and try to take his damn head off. We dare defend ourselves. That should
be your motto. Understand?*

I never pretended—then or now—to embrace a philosophy of
nonviolence though I respected the civil rights leaders who did.

That first year, starting with registration, presented myriad challenges. The assistant principal met with Ettra to review Skinny's
transcripts and discuss the curriculum. Skinny could take one elective
course, and he suggested Home Economics.

"What do they teach in Home Economics?" Ettra posed the
question with all the seriousness she could muster and got an in-kind
reply.

"They are taught cooking, sewing, homemaking, things like
that."

"That's exactly what I thought," Ettra told him. She didn't have to
tell me that she glared at him and did not struggle to mask her anger.
"That's all y'all think we need to learn. I can teach her that at home.
What else do you have to offer?"

"Well, we have band, but—" he hastened to add, "she will have
to buy her own instrument."

"Buying an instrument ain't no problem. Put her in the band,"
Ettra retorted.

SKINNY WANTED A FLUTE.

She offered no reason but I suspected the genes. I have always been
heavy into jazz and my record collection favored pacific jazz sounds
spotlighting the flute. Buddy Collette, the West Coast "Man" for jazz
saxophone and flute, got a lot of repeat play on my turntable, and

anyone in my house got regular doses of his quintet's "Flute Talk" album.

I bought the flute.

"How come y'all bought a flute?" the band director accosted Skinny on her first day of band practice. "Don't you know you can't learn to play that thing? Niggers ain't got flute lips."

When she repeated his insult to me that night, a little bit of pity tinged my anger. This jerk of a teacher clearly didn't know much about band instruments and less about the musicians who mastered them.

I had to chuckle a little, too. Flute lips. I liked that sound, and it quickly replaced "Skinny" as my favorite nickname for Sheryl. Naturally, I reserved it as our private joke.

There would be more incidents in the first year which were no joking matters.

Sheryl boarded the school bus in front of our house for the four-mile trip to school. The bus arrived, and unloaded, minutes before a bell sounded the start of school. While the kids congregated outside, with absolutely no adult supervision, the same band of white boys regularly threw rocks in Sheryl's direction. None had struck her by the time she told me, but I saw no reason to wait for this mischief to escalate from intimidation to assault.

The next morning I parked in my station wagon about a hundred yards from the front entrance of the main building. I watched the bus unload. Nobody threw a single rock. Nonetheless, I decided to alert school officials.

An assistant principal did his best to keep me from talking with the principal. I sat only a short while before the principal appeared to escort me inside his office.

I described the rock-throwing incidents, and he showed as much concern as his chair: "Why don't you just bring your child to school and let her out when the first bell rings, and she won't have to stand outside."

I stood and leaned over his desk to look directly into his eyes.

"The white kids ride the bus—my kid will continue to ride the bus. If you can't put some teachers out there to supervise those kids before first bell and stop the rock throwing, I can stop it."

"Are you telling me you plan to jump on the kids?" His tone suggested he doubted my resolve.

"I won't." Before he could rest assured, I continued. "I'll just stop by Trenholm Court [a public housing project near the police station], pick up half a dozen boys, and drop them off out front about the same time the bus delivers Sheryl."

I didn't need to say more. The principal agreed to assign teachers for "yard duty" to supervise students until they were admitted into the building at first bell. The rock throwing stopped.

About two months later, someone in the principal's office called for me to come right away because "your daughter has a problem." Ushered straight to his office, I darted my eyes over the room: the principal seated behind his desk; the assistant principal and a black staffer standing at his side; a white boy holding a towel to his hand sitting with a woman who appeared to be his mother; Skinny sitting alone in the opposite corner, crying.

I strode right over to Skinny, put my arms around her and told her to be cool, stop crying, and tell me what happened. Between tears she said, "I hit him on the head with my book bag."

"Is he dead?" I asked.

She pointed to the little white boy: "That's him."

I then turned to the principal. "What happened?"

He stated crisply: "Sheryl hit this boy on his head with her book satchel; they were in the hall."

I turned back to my daughter: "Tell us what happened, Sheryl."

She replied that the boy walked up behind her, touched her inappropriately, and said "Hey, black beauty." She turned around and swung her book bag at his head.

Oddly enough, the little fellow did not deny Skinny's account; but he protested that he did not mean any harm.

His response confirmed the correctness of my assessment.

"The problem here is not with Sheryl," I announced. "The problem is with all of the white administrators, faculty, students, and staff at this school who have not yet come to realize that y'all are dealing with a different breed of nigger."

I proceeded to explain that I rejected, for myself and my children, the ideal of nonviolence and that I taught Sheryl to believe in, and act on, her God-given right to defend herself. While I expressed regret about this encounter, I also cautioned them to start preparing for the inevitable droves of future black students who, like Sheryl, absolutely would not tolerate verbal or physical insults.

Whether or not administrators heeded my advice, we witnessed many signs of changing attitudes before Sheryl left Goodwyn for Robert E. Lee High School. In stunning contrast with his junior high predecessor, Lee's band director not only welcomed Sheryl and her flute but also invited us to the band's orientation session. Sheryl played the flute for three years, and her skills helped her garner a band scholarship to Tuskegee University.

"Flute Lips" for sure!

24

The Lake House

S till waters . . . grieving hearts. The mix can be strangely sooth-
ing.

Autumn had barely turned the seasonal page in 1977 when
Ettra and I started our search for some kind of balm to relieve the
agonizing last summer of our third child's life.

Yalise Yvette celebrated her sweet sixteenth birthday on May 27
and only a few weeks later, we were cradling her aplastic anemia-
ravaged body through a gloomy cycle of blood transfusions, doctors,
and hospitals—praying for the miracle which might extend her years
at least beyond our own.

The bone marrow transplant never came, and she left us on September 29. Ironically, her life started only a few months after we bid
farewell, on January 19, 1961, to Michelle Terese, our second-born;
five weeks after her first birthday, she succumbed to cystic fibrosis
diagnosed only by an autopsy.

We spent every weekend for several months exploring lake-front
properties within a short driving distance from our home. One balmy
Sunday morning found us hopefully on the trail of a "for sale" sign
at Lake Jordan.

A surprising disclosure endeared us to the small house immediately:
the owners had a teenage daughter who was Yalise's classmate. It also

helped us to rationalize the obvious shortcomings: a tiny two-tiered cabin, only a fifty-foot frontage, and scarce parking, in the midst of the busiest boat traffic on the main lake. Because we wanted just an occasional weekend retreat, we immediately declared a definite interest in buying the property.

On the next morning I arranged for bank financing and made an afternoon call to the seller's realtor. "That property's been sold, Mr. Seay. I'm sorry, it's no longer on the market."

I knew better. I also knew we would not be satisfied with such a little house. Discrimination finally worked in my favor!

We continued our search on Lake Jordan, this time with help from a realtor.

A few weeks later I drove alone to inspect the realtor's first lead—a densely wooded one-acre lot with the remnants of a burned-out shack fronting 150 feet on the lake. It wasn't the easiest place to find. A young white couple lived year-round in the cabin until a fire destroyed it along with the wife's spirit for rebuilding. I could see a lot of potential in the lot, and I rushed back home to pick up Ettra, silently praying for her approval.

We bought it the next day.

ABOUT NINE O'CLOCK THAT night I answered the phone at home.

"Lawyer Seay?" I detected the youthful voice of a black female.

"This is Judy. Miss Ettra taught me in HeadStart. I work for Mrs. Allen sometimes at her house on Lake Jordan, and she told me to call you. She heard y'all bought some property up there, and she wants to know why since no other colored people live in that area."

I told Judy to let Mrs. Allen know that we had indeed purchased a lot on Lake Jordan. "Now you be sure to tell her," I added, "that we will be there early Saturday morning to pick the site for the house we plan to build."

As soon as we pulled up in Ettra's Lincoln Town Coupe, Mrs. Allen emerged from her little Jim Walter house staked on the hillside about three hundred yards from our lot. When she reached us, she introduced herself cordially enough but the racist tirade which followed belied any welcome.

She just could not understand "why we wanted to buy this property. No colored people live up here. The little fellow who sold you this lot should have come to me first . . . I don't understand why he didn't give me the opportunity to buy it . . . I thought they planned to rebuild the house." She saved her deepest concern for last: that our mere presence in the area would substantially reduce the value of her property.

I spoke up before Ettra could let loose on her. My wife's tongue could be as fierce as her black pride.

"Well, to tell you the truth, we are getting ready to spend $60,000 in the next sixty days to build a house on the side of this hill, and I sure hope your little house won't bring down our investment."

Waving my hands across the lot, I told her she could save her anger for the young sellers. "This was love at first sight," I explained. "I would have topped any offer you made, and if I still lost out, I would be ready to haul you into federal court."

She huffed away shaking her head in utter disbelief.

With Mrs. Allen safely out of earshot, Ettra turned to me. "Did I hear you say $60,000? I thought we were going to build a weekend cabin."

"We were," I replied, "but we ain't no more."

AND SO WE STARTED to build our lake house, a 2,500-square foot, rustic-cedar stand-out. A major squabble with the contractor slowed early construction, and beavers gnawed through landscaping shrubs almost as fast as I planted them.

Several months into the construction, early one Saturday morning, I took my wife, our son, and my lawyer-nephew with me to check on the progress. In shock, dismay, and unadulterated anger, I gazed at three broken window panes in the rear. These thermal panes had been custom-made at considerable expense, and the significant damage would have to be repaired at the factory.

I had no doubt that the rock-throwing culprits were kindred spirits with Mrs. Allen, and I decided in a heartbeat how best to stop her bandwagon.

I headed straight to the Elmore County sheriff's office, ordered Ettra to stay in the car with our fourteen-year-old Quinton, and strode angrily inside, nephew Jimmy in tow. A desk clerk radioed the sheriff that I needed to see him urgently. The hour we waited should have been a sufficient "cooling off" period for my rage, but when the sheriff came in, I was still blowing smoke.

I had remained calm and rational throughout my early practice when hostility and danger constantly assaulted me in countless country towns across the state. Now, clearly out of control, I simply exploded.

I told the sheriff about my encounter with Mrs. Allen and the damaged panes at the lake house.

"I know the white folks don't want me up there, Sheriff, but I am here to stay. From now on, I'm liable to be up here any time of day or night until the house is built. I want you to know that I plan to protect me and my property by any means necessary. I hope I never catch anybody with a rock in his hand, because if I do, you will have to come up there with your meat wagon and drag away a dead ass."

The sheriff remained surprisingly calm. "Seay, you need to just calm down, now. I don't really think you plan to shoot somebody for throwing a rock at your window."

The profanities and expletives which laced my response would have earned a severe tongue-lashing from my mother—even then—and a law enforcement officer unfamiliar with my usual demeanor would have handcuffed me and carted me off to jail.

"You can put a stop to all of this right now, Sheriff, because I know you know who is doing what in your county." Finally regaining a modicum of composure, I beseeched him to put the word out that nobody should mess with me because I had no patience with nonviolence. Of course, I chose more colorful, politically incorrect, and patently offensive language to communicate better just what kind of Negro they were dealing with.

Whatever the sheriff did, if anything, I never experienced another problem at that lake house.

As we walked back to my car, Jimmy gave me a look of awe. "Uncle Solomon," he chuckled, "you know what—you are definitely one crazy Negro."

Thankfully, the good Lord gave me many years after that incident to be sure Jimmy witnessed me in action more worthy of emulation.

PART SIX

JUDGING THE JOURNEY

"Until the lions have their historians, tales of the hunt shall always glorify the hunter."

— *African proverb*

25

REPUTATION

Y**ou are the young fellow who does not like white people."**
It was not a question. Her matter-of-fact tone announced
that she had it on good authority.

Ruth Johnson, widow of the legendary Judge Frank M. Johnson,
Jr., had been on my short list of favorite people for a long time. Much
time had passed since our last meeting, and I looked forward to speaking with her again.

She greeted my wife Ettra so warmly. The two of us had shared quite
a few pleasant encounters with Judge and Mrs. Johnson as his guests
during judicial conferences. So her rebuke to me shocked and stung.
"No, no, no," I responded with all the sincerity I could muster.

We chatted for more than fifteen minutes in the lobby of the
magnificent federal courthouse named in honor of Judge Johnson.
I asked if she still made enough frozen daiquiris on Mondays to last
her all week. Judge joked with me often about how she hoarded her
favorite beverage, believing he never looked inside the freezer. She
gave up the daiquiris about two years prior to his death.

Reminiscing with Mrs. Johnson lifted my spirits that mid-afternoon
in April 2002. Later that evening, though, as I struggled to fall asleep,
my mind wandered through the four decades of my interactions with

Judge Johnson on and off the bench. How did Mrs. Johnson get the impression that I did not like white people?

Did I say or do something in her presence? Had I somehow—somewhere along the way—developed the reputation of a racist? Had Mrs. Johnson given voice to Judge Johnson's belief? The thought annoyed me.

Judge Johnson's opinion mattered to me. Without his courageous court decrees in the 1960s and 1970s, the civil rights movement simply would not have defeated Jim Crow in Alabama. I admired and respected him greatly.

We shared many interesting and candid conversations about race. I never got the impression that he viewed me as a racist. Proudly and fiercely black, to be sure; I left little doubt about my choice of colors and my consistent opposition to racial inequality.

As I pondered whether my plain talk about race matters left a negative impression on Judge Johnson, I remembered his reaction when I appeared fully bearded at a pretrial conference. Coincidentally, for the Alabama Centennial Celebration, the governor asked all men to grow beards in recognition of the state's growth.

"Seay, are you celebrating the Centennial?"

My response to the judge appeared to offend only some of the other lawyers:

"No, sir, I can't rightly say that I grew this beard just to celebrate the Centennial. With all this hoopla, though, I do hope that my beard will remind white folks that they cannot continue to overlook and to deny the many contributions that the black man has made to the growth and development of this great state."

I ALSO REMEMBERED JUDGE Johnson's private talk with me when I became a plaintiff in a federal lawsuit against Governor John Patterson for refusing to renew my license as a notary public.

"Don't you have a secretary to handle notary work, Seay? How does it add anything to your practice to have you as a notary public? Why are you wasting time on this trivial lawsuit?"

True, I seldom used the notary seal before it expired. Not the point, I tried to explain; nothing but racism motivated the governor, and I simply would not tolerate being a victim of racial injustice, regardless of the perpetrator or the damages.

Judge Johnson listened patiently to my outrage. Then he spoke frankly about the retaliation for his unpopular judicial decrees banning segregation. The city took away his on-street parking space; racists regularly shot out the street lights in front of his house, and the power company did not replace them until his neighbors pestered the office with calls.

"Seay," he ended a much longer litany of suffering, "if you are going to be on the forefront in fighting for equal rights, there are some things you just tolerate, and you stay the course."

I persevered with my lawsuit and lost on the governor's motion for summary judgment. The Court of Appeals ruled that Judge Johnson should have given me the chance to prove my allegations at trial. Of course, the governor offered reasons for not renewing my notary license that allegedly had nothing to do with race. When I could not produce evidence sufficient to rebut this trial testimony, again I lost. Judge Johnson presided over the trial without the slightest sign of annoyance with me for pursuing the case.

To THIS DAY I reject any notion that Judge Johnson ever attributed to me any racial hatred for white people. If Mrs. Johnson did not get her impression of me from him, my suspicion shifted to our mutual friend, Virginia Durr.

Virginia's husband, Clifford Durr, was one of the few white lawyers in Alabama who embraced fully—and litigated tirelessly for—the cause of civil rights. The white community generally disdained the Durrs as "race-mixers."

Much more vociferous and outgoing than Clifford, Mrs. Durr frequently attended the weekly mass meetings organized by the Montgomery Improvement Association during the bus boycott. Following the vicious attack on a Greyhound busload of Freedom Riders next to the federal courthouse, an angry Ku Klux Klan mob overturned and burned Mrs. Durr's car after seeing a white woman park it outside the mass meeting at the First Baptist Church on Ripley Street; the car had been borrowed by a journalist friend visiting Mrs. Durr.

The Durrs owned a country home in Elmore County they called Pea Level. There she hosted many racially mixed gatherings, usually spiced with provocative conversations she invariably instigated. Invited for a young white couple's engagement party, Ettra arrived first and explained that I would join her shortly. Mrs. Durr predicted that I would not show up "because he really does not like white people." When I did appear, she expressed her surprise and told me about her prediction.

"No, Mrs. Durr," I corrected her. "I do not dislike white folks, but I do distrust white folks."

"Well, I don't understand you, Sol," she fired back. "Why do you say you distrust whites?"

"If we had done to y'all since 1619 what y'all have done to us, would you trust us?" I rested my case.

I suspect Mrs. Durr interpreted my response as proof that I harbored some abiding hatred for white people. Maybe she communicated as much to Mrs. Johnson.

IN ANY CASE, I realized then and now that somewhere along my journey, I acquired a reputation for disliking white people. It's a reputation that disturbs me because it is absolutely without foundation.

While I have always been fiercely black, I am not now, nor have I ever been, anti-white.

I reflected much that night on my personal and professional relationships with whites over the years.

As early as the mid-1960s I hired a white law student as a research assistant. Enrolled at the University of California in Berkeley, he traveled by motorcycle to Montgomery. Notwithstanding our dramatically different lifestyles, we interacted well together in and out of the office.

For several years I also had a white female associate, a middle-aged divorcee from Seattle, Washington. She appeared as co-counsel in many of my civil rights cases. We traveled together throughout the state, trying cases in every federal court from Huntsville to Mobile and from Dothan to Opelika.

With one exception, I enjoyed a pleasant and professional relationship with all the whites I hired over the years—male and female, law clerks, assistants, associates, and secretaries. The exception underscores the historic obsession of the typical white male with protecting his woman from the stereotypical black buck.

The State Employment Agency sent a relatively young white female to interview for a secretarial vacancy. She had adequate skills, a pleasing personality, and interacted well with our other office personnel. I hired her.

On her second day on the job, a young man came to the office and introduced himself as her husband. He told me he wanted to wait there until she got off for the day. I said, "Fine." He proceeded to sit right in front of her—for approximately three hours.

The next day he showed up again, and he just sat there.

I called his wife into my office. I inquired if she had encountered any problems in the office and if she felt comfortable. She assured me that she felt welcome and enjoyed her work immensely. She apologized for her husband's presence, explaining that he did not feel as comfortable about her work at a black law firm; she needed the job and told me she thought her husband would come around soon.

When he presented himself on the third consecutive day, however, I decided we needed to talk. I invited him into my office and asked him rather frankly whether he had problems with his wife working for us. He responded just as bluntly that he did. She had never worked before, he added, in a totally "colored" environment.

I promptly summoned his wife, thanked her for her work, and told her that her husband's concerns made it best for her to resign immediately. She did.

I left immediately for the State Employment Agency and located the gentleman who referred the secretary. "Don't ever send me another white secretary," I told him without elaboration.

He dutifully lectured me on the legal requirements of the Equal Employment Opportunity Act. Fortunately, neither his reprimand nor my singular experience with this white secretary received any public attention.

I still cannot explain my undeserved reputation for hostility to white people. I just decided not to spend another sleepless night trying to understand.

26

TOLERATED INJUSTICE

Willie V. Dunnigan, the "grossly overweight, dark-skinned man felled by three bullets to his chest"[47] on November 16, 1957, was only forty-four years old. He was a husband to Louise and a father to Manuel, Willie B., Lois, George, Mary Louise, James, Dorothy, and Marie. His first-born son, Manuel, died years before that fateful Saturday night at the family home in Lomax, a tiny black community on the outskirts of Jemison. Just three months earlier the Ku Klux Klan had rampaged through nearby Maplesville, terrorizing any blacks in sight and raiding several homes to run blacks out of town.[48] Word spread quickly. By early November the Klan staked out a rally site in Jemison, and the blacks living up the hill in Lomax expected an invasion soon. Most stockpiled weapons and prepared to defend themselves; Dunnigan did not.

In the aftermath of Dunnigan's death, and the Klan's aggression in Lomax, the Chilton County sheriff arrested most of the town's adult males, keeping me busy for weeks in their defense. More than fifty years would pass before I received a first-hand account of the horrific terror visited on the Dunnigans.

"WELL, MR. SOLOMON, I'VE really tried to put this out of my mind. I've just never been able to come to grips with it all."

A mere eight years old at the time, Dorothy wearily responded to my inquiry. She and Lois, her big sister by five years, had reluctantly agreed to meet me on August 2, 2008, at a Clanton restaurant. They consented only when told of my role as a lawyer for the black men arrested.

I needed to confirm their father's date of death. After poring for weeks through courthouse records and archived newspapers, I connected with an activist from the Chilton County movement who knew the Dunnigans. He arranged this meeting but cautioned that the family never talked about what happened, even among themselves. In fact, a brother who had said he would join us at the restaurant sent word instead that he just could not bear any discussion.

The two sisters had stopped by the Pilgrim Rest Cemetery in Maplesville to record the dates on their father's headstone. They readily authorized me to secure his death certificate, and I marveled that no one had requested it before.

Even with their report and affidavit to secure the official record, I wanted to hear more about that night.

"You can stop anytime you feel the need," I said, trying to assure them that I appreciated the emotional pain of reliving such a horrible episode in their lives. "I just would like to know what happened. We lawyers were so focused on the men in jail, and nobody ever told us what your family went through."

As Lois recalled their terrifying ordeal, all of us took frequent breaks to keep our emotions in check.

"The people in Lomax did talk about the Klan getting ready to do something, but no one knew when or how they would attack."

Lois remembered a banging knock on their door.

"The man yelled for Daddy to let him in, but Daddy didn't open the door. I remember him saying, 'Just go away, I'm not in it.'"

The friend who had introduced me to Dorothy and Lois also knew the man who banged on their door. Ironically, the man had driven to Lomax after sighting Klansmen on the move in that direction. He planned to warn the residents and to help them. When he spied a white mob of uniformed officers, however, he ditched his car and raced up the hill to the Dunnigans' house. Though the man had then left their porch and kept on running, police dogs tracked him to the Dunnigans' door and did not move further.

"After the dogs barked at our door, we could hear people getting closer to the house, and suddenly the house just lit up with those spotlights."

Everything happened quickly. Officers hurled tear gas canisters through the windows and opened fire on the house. Amidst the thunder of rapid gunfire, Lois raced to get under her bed. Her last sighting before taking cover: mother Louise, frantically trying to encircle the other children, took the first shot and fell to the floor.

Lois rose and stretched out her arms to demonstrate.

At that moment I had a flashback to an early episode of Alex Haley's *Roots*. Kunta Kinte's plantation master handed the kidnaped African boy over to Fiddler, a veteran slave, to train Kunta to be a slave with a new name, Toby. Fiddler uttered the greatest line in the whole series: "You in America now, boy."

Before I could fully process this slavery-era image with the reckless shooting of an innocent black mother struggling to shield six little children, Lois returned to her seat and somberly resumed the story.

"When mama got shot, Daddy went outside to try the stop the shooting, and that's when he got shot. I remember Dorothy went running out the door after Daddy."

Flabbergasted, I turned and asked Dorothy why. "All I know," she replied, "is I just ran to get my daddy. The men just kept on shooting, and I saw Daddy fall down."

Dunnigan had no weapons inside the house and carried nothing in his hands. Perhaps he thought the shooters would cease firing when they saw he was not the man they were chasing.

Who were the shooters, I wanted to know. Was it the Klan?

The sisters did not see anybody wearing Klan costumes. Most sported guns and sheriff's uniforms.

Several deputies came inside. The terrified children hovered over their mother's motionless body. An ambulance came to take her to a hospital, and the funeral home sent a car to get their slain father.

"Then they brought us all out of the house and they went back inside. Willie B. managed to escape with Marie, our baby sister. When the deputies came outside, they put me and Dorothy, Mary Louise, George, and James in the back of a sheriff's car and drove us down to the sheriff's office."

Lois heard a single question which dominated the deputies' loud discussions: "What we gon' do 'bout these nigger children?"

The next morning officers brought Willie B. and Marie into the office. They had spent the night in the woods.

Before day's end all seven children were hauled off in another sheriff's car and dropped off on a road near their house.

They started walking to the nearest house. It belonged to Mary Caver. Not related at all to the Dunnigan family, this amazing neighbor listened to their story and lovingly took them in. Upon her discharge from the hospital, with a bullet in her abdomen that never was removed, their mother joined them. "For several years," Lois said, "Miss Caver took care of us, all of us, just like we were her own. We never went back to live in our house."

LOUISE DUNNIGAN, "a loving, caring mother who believed in prayer," died on July 13, 1992. Baby Marie is also dead.

A few days after my meeting with Lois and Dorothy, I linger on three lines penned by the doctor who signed their father's official Certificate of Death:

- Disease or Condition Directly Leading to Death: Gunshot wound of chest
- Time of Injury: Nov. 16, 1957, 10 p.m.
- How did Injury Occur? Shot by police

You were in America, Willie V. Dunnigan, a black man, in Chilton County, Alabama, in 1957.

Liberty and justice? Only for those who got the guts to grab it!

The battle for civil rights is far from over . . . and my soul still stirs to be on the battlefield.

∾

NOTES

Chapter 3, Passing the Bar

1 Paul M. Pruitt, Jr., "The Life and Times of Legal Education in Alabama, 1819-1897: Bar Admissions, Law Schools, and the Profession," 49 *Alabama Law Review* 1–281, 298–303 (1997).

A year before the University of Alabama established its law school, a black graduate of the Law School at Howard University in Washington, D.C., successfully applied for admission to the bar in Mobile, Alabama. J. Clay Smith, Jr., former dean at Howard's law school, records the following account of his admission, printed in the Nov. 22, 1871, edition of the *Mobile Daily Register*:

> Moses Weslydale Moore, a Negro as black as the ace of spades . . . presented himself for examination, stating that he had been admitted to the bar in the District of Columbia. The court requested Judge Gibbons to examine him, and examination was conducted in open court. A great deal of interest was manifested on the part of the bar . . . from the fact of the applicant's color. He passed a very satisfactory examination, and an order was made by the Court admitting him to the bar. This is the first Negro ever admitted to the bar in Mobile.

Citing the *Montgomery Daily State Journal*, Jan. 5, 1872, Smith documents Moore's admission shortly thereafter to the Alabama Supreme Court. J. Clay Smith, Jr., *Emancipation: The Making of the Black Lawyer, 1844–1944,* 271, University of Pennsylvania Press (1993).

2 Birmingham's Howard College, now Samford University, acquired Cumberland and pushed a legislative act extending the diploma privilege to graduates of its law school. Another bill, favored by the Board of Bar Commissioners, would have abolished the privilege except for students enrolled in the University of Alabama Law School as of August 31, 1961. The Board's official action is documented as follows:

> The Secretary, John B. Scott, then briefly reviewed the bills and stated the position of the American Bar Association and the American Association of Law Schools regarding generally the subject of diploma privilege. Upon conclusion of the discussions regarding the new law school and the bills in the Legislature regarding diploma privileges, the following resolution was duly made, seconded

and adopted without dissenting vote:

BE IT RESOLVED by the Board of Commissioners of the Alabama State Bar that it favors legislation whereby all persons applying for admission to the Alabama State Bar be required to pass the State Bar Examination except students enrolled at the University of Alabama Law School as of August 31, 1961.

Minutes of Special Meeting of the Board of Commissioners of the Alabama State Bar, held in the Iron Room of the Tutwiler Hotel, Birmingham, Alabama, July 20, 1961, at 10 A.M.

3   My maternal great-uncle, Arthur H. Madison, graduated from Columbia Law School and gained admission to the Alabama bar on March 10, 1938. His early activism as a civil rights lawyer in Montgomery tragically led to his unfair disbarment. Arthur Davis Shores, admitted to the bar on October 4, 1937, represented Madison in disbarment proceedings. Based on newspaper reports at the time, Dean Smith chronicled this summary of Madison's undoing:

In 1944, while trying to help blacks register to vote, he was arrested under an Alabama statute that made it a misdemeanor to represent a person without his or her consent. Madison had taken appeals for eight blacks who had been denied the right to vote, but "five [of the eight blacks] made affidavits that they had not employed Madison or authorized him to take the appeals. Madison attempted to obtain a legal decision that the restrictive registration law in Alabama was unconstitutional, but the white power structure, led by United States Senator Lister Hill, was adamant that Madison's efforts to register black voters be stopped by whatever means necessary. As a result of Senator Hill's influence and the pressure brought to bear on the Montgomery County Board of Registrars, Madison was disbarred on July 24, 1945. He relocated to New York City.

J. Clay Smith, Jr., *Emancipation: The Making of the Black Lawyer, 1844–1944*, 275, University of Pennsylvania Press (1993); see "Negro Vote Lawyer Put in Jail Here," *Montgomery Advertiser*, April 9, 1944; LaFlore, "Attorney Loses Round 2 in Ala. Disbarment Case," *Chicago Defender*, June 10, 1944; "Illegal Practice Laid to Negro Attorney," *Birmingham News Appeal*, April 11, 1944.

4   Code of Alabama 1958, Tit. 52, § 40 (1)

Authority to provide graduate and professional instruction not available at state-supported educational institutions.

The state board of education, under such rules and regulations as it shall determine, may provide for residents of Alabama graduate and professional instruction not available to them at state-supported educational institutions. The state board of education shall, by its rules and regulations, determine the qualifications of persons who may be aided under this section, and the decisions as to qualifications of persons by the state board of education shall be final. The state board of education may provide such graduate and professional instruction at any educational institution as it deems necessary, within or without state boundaries. The state board of education shall provide such graduate and professional instruction, within the limits of the appropriations available for this purpose, at a cost to students not exceeding the probable cost of such instruction to them if it were offered at a state-supported institution. The state board of education, in providing such instruction, may take into account travel, tuition, and living expenses. (1945, p.61, appvd. June 1, 1945)

5 My future law partners, Charles D. Langford and Fred D. Gray, Sr., were admitted to the Alabama Bar in 1953 and 1954, respectively, and by 1957, the Montgomery Bus Boycott had catapulted their civil rights practice.

Chapter 4, They Must Have Been Brothers

6 "An Ordinance No. 21-57. Be it Ordained by the Board of Commissioners of the City of Montgomery, as follows:

Section 1. It shall be unlawful for white and colored persons to enter upon, visit, use, or in any way occupy public parks or other public houses or public places, swimming pools, wading pools, beaches, lakes or ponds except those assigned to their respective races.

Section 2. It shall be unlawful for any person, who, being the owner, proprietor, keeper or superintendent of any public park or other public houses or public places, swimming pool, beach, lake or pond to allow or knowingly permit white and colored persons to enter upon, visit, use, or in any way occupy a public park or other public houses or public places, swimming pool, wading pool, beach, lake or pond, except those assigned to their respective races.

Section 3. The words 'colored persons', as used herein, shall have the same meaning as 'person of color' as defined in Section 2 of Title 1 of the 1940 Code of Alabama.

Section 4. Any person, firm, corporation or association violating any of the provisions of this ordinance shall be guilty of a misdemeanor against the City of Montgomery, and upon conviction shall be subject to a fine of not more One Hundred Dollars, and imprisonment for not more than six months, one or both at the discretion of the City Recorder.

Section 5. The provisions of this ordinance are severable and should any sentence, paragraph, section or clause of this ordinance be declared unconstitutional by any Court of competent jurisdiction, then such action by said Court shall not affect the other provisions of this ordinance which are otherwise constitutional.

Section 6. Public Health and Public Welfare demanding it, this ordinance shall take effect immediately upon its passage."

7 *Gilmore, et al., etc. v City of Montgomery, et al.*, 176 F. Supp. 776 (M. D. Ala. 1959), aff'd, 277 F. 2d 364 (5th Cir. 1960), rev'd in part and remanded, 417 U.S. 556, 94 S. Ct. 2416, 41 L.Ed. 2d 304 (1974).

8 *Gilmore*, 176 F.Supp. at 780 n.1.

Closed as a result of the Resolution were these parks designated exclusively for Negro citizens—Washington Park, King Hill Park, Trenholm Court Park, and the Mobile Heights Park—and the rest of the public parks reserved for exclusive use of whites and their Negro maids and/or servants while working in those roles: Bear Park, Bruce Field Park, Civic Park, Day Street Park, Diffly Park, Hamner Hall Park, Kiwanis Park, Oak Park, Perry Street Park, and Ridgecrest Park. See *Gilmore*, 176 F. Supp. at 777-78.

The City continued to maintain the parks and to keep some employees on the payroll. The Superintendent of Parks and Recreation "testified . . . there was no 'present intention to reopen the parks during the present term of the incumbent Commissioners,' and . . . that in the event Negroes had presented themselves for admission to those public parks designated for use by whites only prior to the time the parks closed that he would have called the police and would have enforced the ordinance to the best of his ability. Id. at 779.

9   *Gilmore*, 176 F. Supp. at 779-780.

10   *Gilmore*, 176 F. Supp. at 780.

11   "Judge Scott" was none other than Montgomery Recorder's Court Judge John B. Scott, who sentenced Rosa Parks to a $10 fine and court costs after convicting her on December 5, 1955 of violating the ordinance requiring segregated seating on city buses. Judge Scott's great-great-grandfather, General John Scott, co-founded the city of Montgomery.

Chapter 8, Saving PeeWee

12   In the September 28, 1961, opinion rendered on PeeWee's automatic appeal from his conviction, the Alabama Supreme Court summarized the damning, uncontradicted evidence:

Lazenby was killed on January 9, 1960, between the hours of 2:00 and 3:00 P.M. He was shot in the back. Lazenby owned and operated a store in Butler County. At the north end of the store, he had a small office. There was a window on the north side of the office. Lazenby was shot through this window as he sat at his desk working on his books with his back to the window. The bullet passed through the screen on the outside of the window and through a pane in the window, striking Lazenby just under the left shoulder blade, passing through his lung, and lodged near his collar bone.

Prior to his being shot, Lazenby had an argument in the store with the appellant relative to how much groceries the appellant could buy on a credit. The appellant left the store accompanied by two other Negroes. Witnesses testified that the appellant got in a car with a Negro woman and drove away, Other witnesses testified that appellant lived about a mile from Lazenby's store. The two witnesses who accompanied appellant from Lazenby's store testified, in effect, that they met the appellant in the road about one-quarter of a mile from Lazenby's store a few minutes after he left the store with a .22 rile in his hands, and that he was going toward Lazenby's store; that they urged appellant to return to his home and take his rifle with him, but appellant assisted that they go on and not bother him; that while they were talking to appellant the appellant either fired the rifle or it went off; that after the shot was fired in the road, appellant proceeded toward Lazenby's store, and that shortly thereafter these witnesses heard the sound of a shot in the direction of the store.

A clerk in the store testified that when he heard the shot he went immediately to the office and Lazenby was trying to get up out of his chair, that he looked through the window and saw the appellant running away from the store; that he knew the appellant well.

Howard v. State, 273 Ala. 544, 142 So.2d 685 (Ala. 1961).

13 Alabama's 1958 Code governed the indictment; Title 14, § 318 provided:

Any person who is guilty of murder in the first degree shall, on conviction, suffer death, or imprisonment in the penitentiary for life, at the discretion of the jury; and any person who is guilty of murder in the second degree shall, on conviction, be imprisoned in the penitentiary for not less than 10 years, at the discretion of the jury.

14 The Alabama Supreme Court initially denied my "petition to be permitted to file a petition for writ of error coram nobis in the trial court." I based this petition on the systematic exclusion of blacks from PeeWee's grand jury and petit jury. Reasoning that the factual underpinnings for this claim were known, and should have been asserted, at trial, the Court nonetheless denied my petition without prejudice. *Howard v. State*, 275 Ala. 59, 151 So.2d 790 (Ala. 1963). Barely five months later the Court granted the petition on rehearing, explaining:

Originally, we denied Howard's application for leave to file petition for writ of error coram nobis. However, the State, not Howard, filed the application for rehearing in this cause and now appears to take the position that the petition should be granted. Since both parties to this controversy now apparently request that the petition be granted, we accede to the requests.

Howard v. State, 275 Ala. 449, 155 So.2d 927 (Ala. 1963).

Whether or not it mattered, I can not speak with any confidence, but only one fact changed between the Court's April 4, 1963 denial and its September 5, 1963 change-of-heart: Richmond F. Flowers replaced MacDonald Gallion as Alabama's Attorney General, the constitutional officer in charge of criminal appeals from the trial courts.

What I know for sure is this: An incredibly fair-minded and principled trial court judge in the Butler County Circuit Court, Judge T. W. Thagard, allowed me time to amass and present statistical evidence, testimony, and legal arguments to buttress the cited error. His

Judgment on Petition for Writ of Error Coram Nobis, rendered on January 17, 1964, included these pertinent findings and conclusions:

The testimony shows that the Jury Commission that existed at the time of the trial of Petitioner and the new commission appointed in the spring of 1963 have made a conscientious effort to establish a proper balance of white and negro jurors and that this continuing effort has eliminated any imbalance that may have existed in the past. Nevertheless, the proportion of whites and negroes on the jury rolls of Butler County at the time the Petitioner in this case was indicted and tried was about the same as that in the *Seals* case. (*U.S. of America, Ex Rel Willie Seals, Jr. Versus Martin J. Wiman, Warden, Kilby Prison*, Number 19, 391, Fifth Circuit Court of Appeals.

For that reason, the Court finds that the grand jury that indicted Petitioner; and the petit jury that convicted him did not meet the requirements of the United States constitution, as interpreted by the Federal Court, in the *Seals* case, supra, and that, for that reason the defendant is entitled to the relief sought by his petition.

Upon consideration of all of which the Court is of the opinion that there was no evidence of design or intention on the part of the Jury Commissioners to systematically exclude the names of Negroes from the jury box solely because of their color, on the contrary, they actually exerted themselves toward finding legally qualified negroes for jury duty; but, even so, they did not exert themselves sufficiently to meet the requirements laid down by the Fifth Circuit Court of Appeals in the *Seals* case.

It is, therefore, ordered and adjudged by the Court that the judgment of conviction rendered and the sentence imposed by this Court on the Petitioner, Roosevelt Howard, alias PeeWee Howard, on February 23, 1960, be and the same hereby is set aside and annulled; and that the grand jury indictment upon which the Petitioner was tried and convicted be and the same is hereby adjudged void and of no effect.

It is further ordered that said Petitioner be held in the county jail, without bond, to await the action of another grand jury upon the crime of murder with which he is charged in the affidavit supporting the original warrant of his arrest; and that if he is not again indicted within eight months from this date, he be discharged from custody.

Order of January 17, 1964, Ex Parte: *Roosevelt Howard, alias PeeWee Howard, In Re: The State of Alabama v. Roosevelt Howard, alias PeeWee Howard* (Butler County Circuit Court, at Law No. 3686).

Chapter 11, I Cried Real Tears

15 Fred Gray filed against the Macon County Jury Commission one of the first civil actions to remedy systemic exclusion of blacks from jury service: *Mitchell v. Johnson*, 250 F. Supp. 117 (M.D. Ala. 1966).

Chapter 13, Fools Profit from Their Own Mistakes

16 In pertinent part, Title 36, sec. 53 of the Code of Alabama, Recompiled 1958, provided:

> All fines and forfeitures collected upon conviction or upon forfeiture of bail of any person charged with a violation of any of the provisions of this chapter constituting a misdemeanor [including "reckless driving"] shall be, within thirty days after such fine or forfeiture is collected, forwarded to the treasurer."

Testimony from the Justice of Peace confirmed the withholding of fees upon convictions, but "as a matter of practice, where [Justices of Peace did not] convict the defendant, [they did not] get paid."

John Hulett, Plaintiff v. Honorable J. B. Julian, Justice of the Peace, Lowndes County, Alabama, Defendant, The State of Alabama, on the relation of Richmond M. Flowers, as Attorney General of Alabama, Intervenor, 250 F. Supp. 208 (M.D. Ala. 1966).

Chapter 14, The Turkey Bone Warriors

17 *Ronnie Gibbs, et al v City of Eufaula* (No. 11804-N); *Mary Dean Marshall, et al v. City of Eufaula* (No. 11805-N); *Willie Lee O'Bryant, et al v. City of Eufaula* (No. 11807-N); *Benny Weldorne, et al v. City of Eufaula* (No. 11808-N), *Findings and Conclusions* (Unreported decision, M.D. Ala., February 23, 1966)

18 Id.

19 Id., Order, February 25, 1966.

Chapter 15, Cottonreader and the Chinaberry Tree

20 The protests spawned federal litigation which documented the bleak profile for black registered voters in Butler County:

> The total population of Butler County, Alabama, is 24,560 according to the 1960 census: 44.7% of this population is Negro; the voting-age population, according to this census in 1960, was 8,363 white and 4,820 Negro. The statistics available to this Court that have been presented and accepted as true and constituted findings of fact in other cases heretofore determined in this district reflect that as of April, 1964, the total registration of white citizens to vote was 6,905,

of Negro citizens, 525.

R. B. Cottonreader, Rosa Lee Lewis, Fannie Lee Marsh, Margaret Rogers, Charles Cheatham, Emmett Knight, on behalf of themselves and all others similarly situated, v. Elton Johnson, individually and as Mayor of Greenville, Alabama, E.B. Stafford, individually and as Chief of Police of Greenville, Alabama, W. Thomas, individually and as Sheriff of Butler County, Alabama, their agents, servants, employees, successors, and all persons in active concert and participation with them, 252 F. Supp. 492, 494 n. 2 (M.D. Ala. 1966).

21 Approximately 350 to 400 blacks appeared at the Courthouse to register on August 16, and officials managed to register 130 then and another 180 on August 17. *Cottonreader*, id., at 495.

22 As described, in part, in the Memorandum Opinion issued after a hearing on requested injunctions:

> After August the scene in Greenville became and remained relatively quiet until the fall of 1965 when, on November 11, a group of Negroes marched along their usual route from the chinaberry tree to the Butler County Courthouse . . . On this same day some of Cottonreader's group sought to dramatize their cause further by lying in front of and behind one of the school buses that hauled Negro students to the all-Negro attended Greenville Training School. Also on November 11 announcements were made in the school classrooms regarding the parades scheduled for that day; some 25 to 30 Negro students left school to participate in the demonstration.
>
> On Friday, November 12, some of the Negro leaders in the Greenville protest movement again went to the training school. This time they disrupted the classroom activities and assembly exercises by unauthorized entrances and by making announcements concerning the scheduled march for that date. The Negro school authorities lost all control and school was completely disrupted. The demonstrators refused to leave the school. And finally, the police were called.
>
> *Cottonreader*, id., at 495–496.

23 *Cottonreader*, id., at 496.

Chapter 16, Bert & Dan . . . and the Ku Klux Klan

24 Tensions between the black community and police officers had been broiling since and served to fuel the protest movement which emerged from decades of entrenched governmental hostility to equal rights for black citizens in Autauga County. See *Houser v. Hill*, 278 F. Supp. 920, 925 (M.D. Ala. 1968); see, e.g., id. at 923, n.3 (detailing federal lawsuits required (a) to compel county Board of Registrars to open registration records to U.S. Attorney General investigating racial discrimination, and (b) to remedy an "il-

legal and unconstitutional regulation" by the State Department of Pensions and Security which removed "a substantial number of Negro children" from the Aid to Dependent Children rolls in Autauga County)

25 *Houser v. Hill*, 278 F. Supp 920, 924, Appendix C (M.D. Ala. 1968). Sandra Colvin, a witness at the federal hearing convened four months after this altercation, detailed this encounter, and the court admitted into evidence her contemporaneous notes, which have been slightly edited here for clarity.

26 The court accepted as "credible" and included as Appendix A the testimony of 16-year old Nitricia Hadnott regarding these events. Her mother, Sallie Hadnott, a civil rights veteran, joined Houser as a named plaintiff in the class action lawsuit which resulted from this protest. See *Houser v. Hill*, 278 F. Supp 920, 924 (M.D. Ala. 1968).

27 *Houser v. Hill*, id. at 925.

28 Id.

29 Judge Johnson found that neither Carmichael's "Black Power" shouts nor the response by protestors justified excessive police force:

> [T]here was no evidence that the meeting was unruly or was creating any disturbance when the defendant city officers continued to remain at the meeting, there was no showing that there was any clear and present danger of any disorder, disturbance or interference with traffic upon the public streets, or any other immediate threat to public safety. However, this Court is convinced that, after the meeting had been disturbed by the officers without sufficient justification and had been removed to Dan Houser's residence, after the initial shots were fired and in response to the illegal and "high-handed" conduct of the city officers, some of the Negro citizens who were there in attendance armed themselves with shotguns, rocks and other weapons for the purpose of harassing, and did harass, on the night of June 11, the police officers and other citizens in cars in or near the Happy Hollow area.
> *Houser v. Hill*, id. at 926.

Chapter 17, *The Other Side of the Battle*

30 The Alabama Legislature, in 1927, codified these definitions for the African American race then commonly identified as Negroes:

> The word "negro" includes mulatto.
> The word "mulatto" or the term "person of color" means a person of mixed blood descended on the part of the father or mother from negro ancestors, without reference to or limit of time or number of generations removed.

Previously, according to the Editor's Note, "a person was a 'negro' if descended on the part of the father or mother from negro ancestors, to the fifth generation inclusive, although one ancestor of each generation may have been a white person." See Code 1923, § 2 (5).

Code of Alabama 1940(Recomp. 1958), § 2 (1927, p. 716; 1951, p.551, appvd. July 19,1951).

31 The 2000 Census documents the black population as 92.7% of the 878 total, a median household income of $17,589, and a median house value of $43,000.00.

32 *Veldhousen v. Burton, etc., et al.*, CV80M 0511 E, (N.D. Ala. ,April 21, 1980) (Complaint, ¶4 at 2).

33 The designated defendants, sued in individual and official capacities, were Colonial Burton, Omilered Ball, Jr., and Reverend Otis Mallory.

34 The only school in Hobson City, the "C.E. Hanna School," included only grades 4 and 5 and for many years, it remained an all-black school. Public school desegregation transferred it from the Calhoun County to the Oxford City school system, where it is now a predominantly white school with slightly under 500 students.

Chapter 18, Freedom Riders and a Slow Delivery

35 My mother's sister, Frankie Madison, married John H. Winston, Sr. Uncle John, fondly called Professor Winston outside the family, never missed a single day as a teacher for more than twenty years at Montgomery's Carver High School. A son, Dr. John H. Winston, Jr., continues to practice medicine in the capital city.

36 Judge Frank M. Johnson, Jr.'s description of this confrontation follows:

> A serious riot occurred at the Greyhound bus station in Montgomery, Alabama, on May 20, 1961. This incident occurred after an interracial group, known as "freedom riders," arrived in Montgomery with the announced purpose of testing the bus facilities in Montgomery to determine whether the facilities could be used without any discrimination on account of race or color.
>
> There was a crowd around the bus station as the bus arrived. After the bus parked to unload its passengers, the Greyhound bus driver announced over the loud speaker system, "Here comes the 'freedom riders' to tame the South."
>
> Some of the crowd then attacked the "freedom riders." General disorder broke out and during the following two hours a number of 'freedom riders' and innocent Montgomery Negroes were injured by the mob. The police were not on the scene at the time the bus arrived.*
>
> *n1. A more detailed discussion of the facts surrounding the May 20, 1961, riot may be found in this Court's opinion in *United States v. U.S. Klans, et al.*, No.

1718-N, D.C., 194 F. Supp. 897, 901. In that case, this Court specifically found "that the Montgomery Police Department . . . willfully and deliberately failed to take measures to ensure the safety of the students and to prevent unlawful acts of violence upon their persons." This lack of protection on the part of the city police of Montgomery continued even after the arrival of the bus. The Court's order of June 2, 1961, restrained and enjoined the Montgomery Police Department from "willfully failing to provide police protection for persons traveling in interstate commerce in and through Montgomery, Alabama."

Lewis, et al., et cet., v. The Greyhound Corporation, et al., 199 F. Supp. 210, 211 (M.D. Ala. 1961).

The named plaintiffs in this class action were John R. Lewis [the Troy, Alabama native who, in 1986, became a revered congressman from Georgia], Paul E. Brooks, Lucretia R. Collins, Rudolph Graham, Catherine Burks, Matthew Petway, and Ralph D. Abernathy [Dr. King's successor as president of both the Montgomery Improvement Association and the Southern Christian Leadership Conference].

In addition to the Greyhound Corporation, these defendants were joined: Capital Motor Lines; Continental Crescent Lines, Inc.; Earl James, L. B. Sullivan, and Frank Parks, individually and as members of the Board of Commissioners of the City of Montgomery, Alabama; and Goodwin J. Ruppenthal, individually and as Chief of Police of the City of Montgomery, Alabama; MacDonald Gallion, individually and as Attorney General of the State of Alabama; and C.C. (Jack) Owen, J.S. Foster and Sibyl Pool, individually and as members of the Alabama Public Service Commission; and Mac Sim Butler, individually and as Sheriff of Montgomery County, Alabama..

Ten Intervenors in the lawsuit—George Smith, Joseph Charles Jones, Wyatt T. Walker, Bernard Lee, Fred L. Shuttlesworth, Clyde Carter, William S. Coffin, John Maguire, David Swift and Gaylord Noice—had been arrested on May 25 after trying to integrate the lunch counter at the Trailways Bus Terminal.

37   For almost half of the forty-two years she practiced family medicine, Dr. Wilson remained the only black female doctor in town. One of only two blacks in her 1953 class at the Women's Medical College of Pennsylvania, she came home in 1958 and nurtured six children of her own (including three medical doctors) while compassionately serving not only primarily poor patients but also the movement's victims and underserved children.

38   St. Jude's Catholic Hospital, located at the intersection of Fairview Avenue and Oak Street, served black patients and black physicians from its opening in 1951 until its closing in 1985. To secure medical care at the city's other Catholic hospital at the time, the downtown-located St. Margaret's, black patients were relegated to a poorly maintained outbuilding detached from the main hospital.

39   Like many, many children of the post-bus boycott movement for whom the Montgomery Improvement Association's weekly mass meetings were as routine as daily school, Delores

R. Boyd—then barely a month past her eleventh birthday—huddled happily in the basement and occasionally peeked at the curious sights outside the window.

40 Just six months shy of his forty-first birthday when we met, Percy E. Sutton was a flyer during World War II and served with the Tuskegee Airmen. He cemented his national stature as a civil rights lawyer, President of the Manhattan Borough, and founder of a broadcasting empire in New York. Mark Lane considered himself a Sutton protégé as a lawyer for social activists and controversial figures, but he is perhaps best known for his controversial books on the assassination of President John F. Kennedy.

41 Judge Johnson recited these evidentiary findings:

>On May 24, the "freedom riders" who had arrived on the 20th went to the Trailways bus station in Montgomery, were served at the white lunch counter, boarded a Trailways bus and departed for Jackson, Mississippi. They were accompanied by a heavy convoy of national guardsmen.
>On May 25, ten individuals, including both whites and Negroes, were arrested by Montgomery County Sheriff Mac Sim Butler at the white lunch counter in the Trailways Bus Terminal in Montgomery on charges of breach of the peace and conspiracy. These arrests were made by the sheriff under specific directions from the National Guard Commander, General Graham. Prior to their arrests, some of them had purchased tickets to Jackson, Mississippi. The group was taken to and confined in the jail.
>*Lewis v. Greyhound Corp.*, 199 F. Supp at 212.

Chapter 19, Marengo County

42 Along with *Lee v Macon County Bd of Educ.,* 221 F. Supp. 297 (M.D. Ala. 1963) and 267 F. Supp. 458 (M. D. Ala. 1967), Fred filed similar class actions to desegregate public school systems in the counties of Barbour, Bullock, Crenshaw, and Montgomery. His autobiography, *Bus Ride to Justice—Changing the System By the System: The Life and Works of Fred Gray* (NewSouth Books, 2000), offers unique insights on the course of this seminal litigation.

43 *Brown v. Bd. of Educ.* (Brown I), 347 U.S. 483 (1954); *Brown v. Bd. of Educ.*(Brown II), 349 U.S. 294 (1955).

44 Managing all ninety-nine cases overwhelmed the initial court of three federal judges (Circuit Judge Richard T. Rives, District Judges Hobart Grooms and Frank M. Johnson, Jr.), and they soon transferred each case to the federal judicial district of the location for school systems involved in each case.

45 The all-black Alabama State Teachers Association (ASTA) successfully intervened in the *Lee v. Macon* litigation, in 1967, to protect the interests of black faculty and staff. Upon

its merger with the all-white Alabama Education Association, ASTA ceased to exist, but the National Education Association agreed to continue its participation in the litigation as a plaintiff-intervenor.

(See *Lee v. Macon*, Civil Action No. 604-E, U.S. District Court for the Middle District of Alabama; Orders dated September 20, 1967, and August 21, 1969).

46 Letter dated September 4, 1974, directed to "Mr. Wayne Witkowshi, Attorney—Education Section, U.S. Department of Justice, Washington, D.C. 20530," from "Fred D. Ramsey, Superintendent—Marengo County School System." The letter indicates copies to "President Ford, Attorney General William Saxbe, District Judge W. Brevard Hand, Senator James Allen, Senator John Sparkman, Representative Walter Flowers, Stanley Pottinger, Brian K. Landsberg, Thomas Keeling, Solomon Seay, Hugh Lloyd, Board Members, Principal of Marengo High School, Trustees of Marengo High School."

Chapter 26, Tolerated Injustice

47 See "Facing Fear," Chapter 9.

48 Chilton County was a stronghold for the Ku Klux Klan in the 1950s, but the summer of 1957 erupted in significant violence by Klan chapters against blacks throughout the state, especially in Jefferson, Mobile, and Montgomery counties. A newspaper reporter (Stuart Culpepper, "Ku Klux Klan Upsets Peaceful Town," *Montgomery Advertiser-Journal*, August 18, 1957) covering the Klan's August 1957 raids in Maplesville underscored the audacious belligerence which made the Klan so feared during this period. According to the newspaper article, an anonymous caller phoned the Maplesville police chief with a warning on August 9, 1957: "There is going to be a meeting of the Ku Klux Klan in your town tonight." The report continued:

> . . . At 7 *p.m.* a caravan of approximately 35 cars cruised into the main street carrying four and five men in each vehicle. Suddenly the sleepy little town of 850 residents, predominantly white, burst into a state of shock and fear.
>
> The cars' passengers spilled out into the street and began donning white robes and hoods. Once costumed, the troublemakers began a march through the town that will long be remembered by those who witnessed it.
>
> . . . The mysterious group, estimated to be about 150 to 200 men strong, paraded through the town twice and left—or so it appeared.
>
> . . . After leaving the main street the Klansmen stopped for visits at several Negro homes. Marching into one house, brandishing "long guns, some of them army automatics," they told its owner to "pack up and get out!"
>
> "I had been there in that little house for 22 years," said Pearlee Goree, "but I figured I'd better get out, since they said I couldn't live there no more."
>
> Striding into Will Brown's home, they yanked him out of the bed to which he had been confined on and off for the last four months. They beat him over

the head with a bottle and commanded, "Get out of town by Monday night." Brown had lived there all his life and was an old man. He had never bothered anybody, said the Mayor.

Will Brown left town the next day, heading for north Alabama. Two more Negro families followed him in the next two days.

Five other Negroes were beaten with rubber hoses and "what looked like leather black jacks." They were in the backyard of Pearlee's brother's house, waiting for a football game to start on television.

. . . Three prominent Maplesville people have publicly defended the Negroes of the town, deploring the "revolting action of the Klan." One of them, a veneer mill operator, has had his life threatened.

. . . Chilton County Sheriff Hugh Champion was not even notified of the Klan violence for a full 24 hours after it had happened.

INDEX

A

Abbott, Police Chief 67
Abernathy, Juanita 85
Abernathy, Rev. Ralph D.
 xviii, 144
 and 1961 Freedom Ride
 riots 83, 85
Admiral Semmes Hotel,
 Mobile 23, 25
African Methodist Episco-
 pal Zion Church xviii,
 33, 101
Agricultural Adjustment Act
 of 1938 105
Alabama Bar Association
 segregation at annual
 meetings 23–28
Alabama Centennial Cel-
 ebration 124
Alabama Court of Criminal
 Appeals 51–53
Alabama Department of Ar-
 chives and History xxii
Alabama Education Associa-
 tion 146
Alabama Law Review 134
Alabama Public Service
 Commission 144
Alabama state bar exam
 11–13, 134–147
Alabama State College.
 See Alabama State
 University
Alabama State Employment
 Agency 127
Alabama State Legislature
 52
Alabama State Teachers As-
 sociation 145

Alabama State University
 57, 111
Alabama Supreme Court
 11, 134
Allen, James 146
American Association of
 Law Schools 134
American Bar Association
 134
Armstrong, Rev. Louis 18
Arter, A. O. 8
Autauga County Improve-
 ment Association 75
Autauga County Voters As-
 sociation 75

B

Ball, Omilered, Jr. 143
Barbour County 63
Belser, T. A. 18
Billingsley, Orzell 44
Black Panthers, The 59
Board of Commissioners of
 the City of Montgomery
 136
boycotts (as means of civil
 protest) 63–68
Boyd, Delores R. 144
 interviewing and bio-
 graphing of Solomon
 Seay, Jr. xx–xxiv
 professional develop-
 ment of xvii–xix
Brooks, Paul E. 144
Brown, Charlotte Hawk-
 ins xv
Brown, Elizabeth 17
Brown v. Board of Education
 xx, 12, 89
Brown, Will 146

Burks, Catherine 144
Burton, Colonial 143
Butler County 70, 102,
 140
Butler, Mac Sim 84–86,
 144, 145

C

Calhoun County 79, 143
Capital Motor Lines 144
Cargill, Mattie 17
Carlton, Gussie 17
Carmichael, Stokely 59,
 70, 76–78
Carter, Clyde 144
Carter, Eugene 29–30
Carver Elementary School,
 Montgomery 111
Caver, Mary 132
Champion, Hugh 147
Cheatham, Charles 141
Chilton County 40–44,
 45–47, 129
 and Ku Klux Klan
 146–147
Civil Rights Act of 1964
 21, 23
Clanton 40
Clark, James E. 28
Clayton 63, 65
Coffin, William Sloane
 86–87, 144
Cole, Harry 26
Collins, Lucretia R. 144
Columbia Law School 135
Colvin, Sandra 142
Conley, Charles xx
Continental Crescent Lines
 144
cotton farming 105–107

Cottonreader, R. B. 70–73
Culpepper, Stuart 146
Cumberland Law School 11

D

Daddy Bone 63–64
Dannelly Field 67
death penalty 33, 138
DeMent, Ira 65
demonstrations. *See* voting rights demonstrations
1967 Prattville Black Power demonstration 76–78
Demopolis City Schools 90
Demopolis Hotel 95
desegregation xviii
of public schools xx, 89, 111
resistance to 91
Dickerson, Mahala Ashley xx
Dunnigan, Dorothy 129–133
Dunnigan, George 129, 132
Dunnigan, James 129, 132
Dunnigan, Lois 129–133
Dunnigan, Louise 129–133
Dunnigan, Manuel 129
Dunnigan, Marie 129, 132
Dunnigan, Mary Louise 129, 132
Dunnigan, Willie B. 129, 132
Dunnigan, Willie V. 129–133
Durr, Clifford 84, 126
Durr, Virginia 84, 126

E

Elite Cafe 21–22
eminent domain 54–56
Equal Employment Op-
portunity Act 128
Eufaula 63–68

F

First Baptist Church, Montgomery 126
and 1961 Freedom Ride riots 83
and Montgomery Improvement Association xviii
First Baptist Church, Prattville 76
First National Bank 26
Flowers, Richmond 138, 140
Flowers, Walter 146
Ford, Gerald 94, 146
Foster, J. S. 144
Freedom Riders 82–88, 145
1961 assault on in Montgomery xviii, 143

G

Gallion, MacDonald 138, 144
Gayle, W. A. 16–20
Gibbons, Judge 134
Gibbs, Ronnie 140
Gilmore, Georgia 17
Gilmore, Mark 14–20
Godbold, John C. xix
Goodwyn Junior High School, Montgomery 111
Goree, Pearlee 146
Graham, Rudolph 144
Graves, Hamp 64
Gray, Fred xix, xx, 27, 44, 49, 136, 140, 145
and 1961 Freedom Ride riots 83, 86
and public school desegregations 89
autobiography of 145
president of Alabama State Bar Association 28
Gray, Langford, and Seay, Law Firm xvii xix
and desegregation of public schools 89
Green, George 59
Greensboro xiv, 102
Greenville 33, 69
Greyhound Bus Co. 143
Grooms, Hobart 145

H

Hadnott, Sallie 142
Haley, Alex 131
Hand, W. Brevard 146
Hanna (C. E.) School 143
Harris, Fred 17
Heart of Camden Motel 96
Hill, James Fitts 18
Hill, Kenneth "Kennedy" 76–78
Hill, Lister 135
historically black schools xv
Hobson City 79–81, 143
Hood, James 11
Hope, Jack 18
Houser, Dan 75–78, 141
Houston, Charles Hamilton 12
Howard College. *See* Samford University
Howard Law School xx, 12, 26 134
Howard, Roosevelt "Pee-Wee" 34–39, 137–147
Howard University xvi
Hulett, John 57–59

J

Jackson Hospital, Montgomery 14
James, Earl 144
jazz xvi
Jefferson County
    and Ku Klux Klan 146
Jefferson Davis Hotel, Montgomery 25
Jemison 40, 129
Jim Crow 124
    and public water fountains 29
    in Alabama Bar Exam 11–12
    in jury selection 48–53
Johnson, Elton 141
Johnson, Frank M., Jr. xix, 67–68, 73, 77, 96, 104, 123–125, 142, 143, 145
    and desegregation of Montgomery public parks 18–20
Johnson, Lyndon 21, 23
Johnson, Ruth 123
Johnson, Sylvia 17
Jonah 5
Jones, Joseph Charles 144
Jordan, Mollie 52
Julian, J. B. 140
justices of the peace 58

K

Keeling, Thomas 146
Kennedy, John F. 145
Kilby Prison 35
King, Dr. Martin Luther xviii, 23, 70
Knight, Emmett 141
Knoxville 102
Ku Klux Klan 40–44, 45–47, 78, 126, 129–133, 146–147
    and 1961 Freedom Ride riots 84

L

Lake Jordan 57, 116–120
Landsberg, Brian K. 146
Lane, Mark 84, 145
Langford, Charles xix, xx, 136
Lanier (Sidney) High School, Montgomery 111
Lazenby, Vandiver 34–39, 137
Lee, Bernard 86, 144
Lee County 55
Lee (Robert E.) High School, Montgomery 111
Lee v. Macon County Board of Education 89, 91, 97
Lewis, John R. 144
Lewis, Rosa Lee 141
Linden City Schools 90
Livingstone College xv
Lloyd, Hugh 95, 146
Lomax 129
Lomax Hannon School, Greenville 33, 102
Loveless Junior High School xviii
Lowndes County 48, 57
Lowndes County Freedom Organization 59
Lumpkin, Norman 77

M

Macon County 105
Madison, Arthur H. 135
Madison, Carrie. *See* Seay, Madison Carrie
Madison, Frankie (aunt) 143
Madison Park 33, 35, 57, 87, 111
Maguire, John 144
Mallory, Otis 143
Malone, Vivian 11

Manhattan Borough 145
Mantz, Bob 59
Maplesville 129, 146
Marengo County 89–98
Marengo County Schools 90
Marshall, Mary Dean 140
Marsh, Annie Lee 141
Mobile County
    and Ku Klux Klan 146
Mobile Daily Register 134
Montgomery xiv, 144
    Parks and Recreation Board 15–20
    school system 111
    segregation laws 136
Montgomery Advertiser-Journal 146
Montgomery Bus Boycott xviii, 14, 136
Montgomery Country Club 25
Montgomery County
    and Ku Klux Klan 146
Montgomery County Bar Association 101
Montgomery County Board of Registrars 135
Montgomery Daily State Journal 134
Montgomery Improvement Association xviii, 106, 144
Moore, Moses Weslydale 134
Mount Zion A.M.E. Zion Church, Montgomery 102

N

NAACP 52
    Legal Defense Fund xix, 27, 58
National Education Association 95, 146

Noice, Gaylord 144
North Carolina xiv, 102
Nussbaum, Bertha 74–78

O

Oak Park, Montgomery 14–20
O'Bryant, Willie Lee 140
Opelika 54
Opelika Housing Authority 54
Owen, C.C. "Jack" 144
Oxford City 143

P

Palmer Memorial Institute xv
Parks, Frank W. 17, 144
Parks, Rosa 137
Patterson, John 125
Petway, Matthew 144
picketing (as means of civil protest) 64–68
plantation farming 33, 105
police brutality 79–81, 129–133
Pool, Sibyl 144
Pottinger, Stanley 146
Price, Charles 101
Pruitt, Paul M., Jr. 134
Pryor, Calvin xx, 12

R

racial discrimination
and racial terminology 142
in judicial proceedings 49
in real estate practices 117
Rafferty, M. J. 18
Ramsay, Fred D. 90, 91, 94, 97–98, 146
Rives, Richard T. 145
Rogers, Margaret 141

Roosevelt, Theodore xxiii
Roots 131
Ruppenthal, Goodwin J. 144

S

Salisbury, North Carolina xv
Samford University 134
Saxbe, William 146
Scott, Gen. John 137
Scott, James E. 27
Scott, John B. 134, 137
Seay, Carrie Madison (mother) 33, 107
Seay, Ettra (wife) xvi, 21–22, 23–28, 103, 109, 110, 112, 117–118, 123, 126
pregnancy with and birth of Yvette Yalise Seay 83, 86, 87
Seay, Michelle Terese (daughter) 116
Seay, Noble 102
Seay, Quinton Spencer (son) 21
Seay, Sheryl Denise (daughter) 110–115
Seay, Solomon S., Jr. xix, 101, 146
xix–xx
and 1961 Freedom Ride riots 82–88
and 1966 Eufala commercial boycotts 64–68
and cotton farming 105
and efforts against discriminatory jury selection 48–53
and eminent domain practices 54–56
and Greenville voting rights demonstra-

tions 70–73
and Mark Gilmore suit 14–20
and police brutality cases 79–81
and public school desegregation 89–98
and The Ku Klux Klan 40–44, 45–47
anti-white reputation of 123–133
attempted shooting of 108–109
Seay, Solomon Snowden Sr., Rev. (father) xvi, 33, 101
and cotton farming 105–107
as Montgomery Improvement Association president 106
relationship with Delores Boyd xvii–xviii
shooting of 108–109
Seay, Yalise Yvette (daughter) 21, 103
birth of 88
death of 116
Sedalia, North Carolina xv
segregation
and racial terminology 142
in Alabama law schools 11
in public parks 14–20
in Public Transportation xv
of Alabama State Bar 23–28
of judicial buildings 36
of public school system 89, 111
Sellers, Clyde C. 16, 18
Selma to Montgomery March 74

Shores, Arthur Davis 135
Shuttlesworth, Fred L. 86, 144
Smith, George 144
Smith, J. Clay, Jr. 17, 134, 135
Southern Christian Leadership Conference 70–73, 144
Southern Courier, The 77
Sparkman, John 146
Spencer, Ettra. *See* Seay, Ettra (wife)
Stafford, E.B. 141
Steiner, Robert E., III 26
Stephens, George 17
St. Jude's Hospital, Montgomery 83, 144
Strassburger, Florian 18
Student Non-Violent Coordinating Committee (SNCC) 58–59, 75
1966 Eufala boycotts 63–68
Sullivan, L. B. 144
Sullivan v. New York Times xxiii
Sutton, Percy 84, 145
Swift, David 144

T

Tennessee 102
Thagard, T. W. 35–39, 138
Thomas, Barbara 26–28
Thomas, Daniel H. 91
Thomaston 92
Thomas, William H. 26, 141
Trenholm Court housing project 114
Tuskegee Airmen, The 145
Tuskegee University 115
Tutwiler Hotel, Birmingham 135

U

Underwood, Jefferson, M.D. 108
University of Alabama Law School 11, 134
automatic bar admission for graduates 134–135
University of California 127
University of Virginia xix
urban development 54–56
U.S. Department of Justice 91

V

Veldhousen, Ronald L. 79–81
Vietnam War 77
voter registration 58–59, 63–65, 71
voting rights demonstrations 69–73

W

Walker, Wyatt T. 86, 144
Wallace, George C. 11, 63
Wallace, Gerald 65
Weldorne, Benny 140
White Hall community 59
Whitfield Pickle Company 107
Whitley Hotel, Montgomery 25
Wilson, Hagalyn Seay, M.D. 88, 144
and 1961 Montgomery Freedom Ride riots 82
relationship with Delores Boyd xvii
Wilson, James (nephew) 109, 119–120
Winston, John H., Jr. (cousin) 143

Winston, John H., Sr. (uncle) 82, 143
Witkowshi, Wayne 146
Women's Medical College of Pennsylvania 144
Wood, Phillip 78
WVAS radio station 57

Y

Yale University 86